RAND

Change in Taiwan and Potential Adversity in the Strait

Evan A. Feigenbaum

Prepared for the
Office of the Secretary of Defense

National Defense
Research Institute

The following report on Taiwan has been produced under the aegis of a project entitled *Reevaluating Asia: Regional Indicators and U.S. Policy.* This project in its entirety represents a multi-year effort to analyze the political-military, social, and economic dimensions of change in the Asia-Pacific region. In particular, the research identifies medium- and long-term trends and developments, highlighting those that might be potentially adverse to U.S. interests in that region. The goal of the project is to delineate a set of key indicators within the various dimensions, an indicator being an event, process, or development that portends possible changes with negative implications for core U.S. policy assumptions and regional security objectives.

Research products for *Reevaluating Asia: Regional Indicators and U.S. Policy* include a regional overview report (forthcoming) as well as three country-specific reports that focus on domestic change and its effect on the Asia-Pacific region and U.S. policy toward the region. This report on Taiwan is one of the country-specific reports. The two other documents focus on China and Japan. They are: MR-605-OSD, *China: Domestic Change and Foreign Policy,* by Michael D. Swaine, 1995; and MR-616-OSD, *Japan: Domestic Change and Foreign Policy,* by Mike M. Mochizuki, 1995.

This research was sponsored by the Office of the Under Secretary of Defense for Policy. It was carried out under the auspices of the International Security and Defense Policy Center within RAND's National Defense Research Institute (NDRI), a federally funded research and development center sponsored by the Office of the Secretary of Defense, the Joint Staff, and the defense agencies.

The author is a visiting fellow at the Center for International Security and Arms Control, Stanford University, and a RAND consultant.

CONTENTS

FIGURES

TABLES

Taiwan recently upset a relatively delicate balance in the cross-Strait relationship through a series of dramatic moves, capped by the June 1995 visit of President Lee Teng-hui to a Cornell University reunion. These moves have been perceived in Beijing as a direct provocation, and in the most recent cycle of Taiwanese provocation and Chinese overreaction, there thus exists potential for mutual miscalculation, real crisis, and perhaps even armed conflict. These potential dangers have arisen largely in response to a long-term process of change within Taiwan and between Taiwan and the mainland.

- The domestic context of Taiwan's foreign and security policies has been thoroughly altered by more than a decade of fundamental social and political change. The old Nationalist Party (KMT) mandarins from the mainland are gone, replaced by a new generation raised and rooted on the island. Most of this generation takes de facto independence as a given in discussing Taiwan's future. Although the question of de jure independence remains contentious, Taiwan's leaders no longer view the mainland as an ideological and political antagonist in the struggle for control of China but as an *external* threat that must be deterred and balanced in the interests of Taiwan's security.

- The above changes in attitude reflect an emerging popular and political consensus that Taiwan's identity is distinct from that of China. This belief is also influenced by a transformation of the political system into a contest between locally oriented parties and increasing confidence on the island in Taiwan's ability to leverage wealth, offshore investment, foreign exchange reserves, and international capital flows for political and diplomatic gain.

But significant constraints on Taiwanese moves toward independence remain:

- Internally, democratization has made it difficult for any party in Taiwan to upset the status quo in the absence of broad popular support. A short election cycle forces parties to seek public legitimation frequently and lends the character of referenda to most polls, checking tendencies toward bold (and potentially dangerous) policy shifts, and promoting incrementalism. Moreover, the diversification and expansion of local interest groups mean that not merely KMT interests, but also opposition Democratic Progressive Party (DPP) interests, potentially conflicting business interests, and a variety of social interests have distinct, and often irreconcilable, stakes in Taiwan's mainland policy. These trends suggest the unlikelihood of sweeping or sudden policy shifts, despite a frequent use of provocative political rhetoric.

- Externally, Taiwan remains highly trade dependent. Moreover, the slow pace of its attempt to create a more capital and technology-intensive economy means that any conflict with China would severely jeopardize both overseas investments and this larger restructuring effort. A cross-Strait conflict would thus force a trade-dependent Taiwan to jettison its focus on the very issues most crucial to its future prosperity and growth. Moreover, China's explicit threat of force in the event of a Taiwanese independence declaration means that Taiwan cannot take for granted China's likely response to any dramatic policy shift.

- Taiwan's primary foreign policy strategy is designed to strengthen popular support domestically by increasing the island's profile abroad while simultaneously avoiding provocations of Beijing. But given China's harsh reaction to every Taiwan effort to raise its profile abroad, this is a dangerous line to walk.

Taiwan must therefore balance rhetorical posturing with policy substance. It cannot posture too loudly without provoking the Chinese. Yet electoral politics forces parties and candidates to forcefully stand up for the island's interests.

The primary danger to the present status quo is thus that either Beijing or Taipei will miscalculate or misread the other's moves. Taiwanese political posturing might be read in Beijing as substantively significant, thereby provoking a Chinese response. At the same time, China's bluster and harsh reaction to each and every attempt to increase Taiwan's overseas profile might be read in Taipei as a bluff, leading Taiwan's leaders to push harder and thereby move beyond actions that China is likely to tolerate.

The crucial balance in the relationship is thus between what Taiwan will or will not do in its interest and what China can or cannot try to impose. *Avoiding miscalculations is the key to avoiding short- to medium-term conflict.*

For the United States, this implies:

1. Mixed statements of U.S. policy contribute to the possibility of miscalculation. If the United States speaks with more than one voice, each side may act only on the basis of what it chooses to hear. For this reason, greater coordination between the executive branch and the Congress is necessary. Moreover, coordination with Beijing on the Taiwan issue will probably prove easier than with Taipei, since Taiwan's democratization means that the regime relies on popular consensus, whereas Beijing can more easily formulate, coordinate, and implement mutually agreed-upon policies. This factor reinforces the need for the United States to speak to Taiwan with a single voice.

2. The U.S. position on Taiwan's status must be made clear to the Taiwanese. Taipei should be left with no ambiguity as to the U.S. position that only a peaceful, *mutually agreeable* solution among the two parties is an acceptable basis for a change in the status quo. Unilateral moves by Taiwan toward de jure independence, including high-profile memberships in Inter-Governmental Organizations, do not square with present U.S. policy.

3. The Taiwan issue is intimately related to the broader U.S. strategic relationship with Beijing. U.S. policy toward Taiwan should therefore be firmly placed in the context of this broader Sino-American relationship. Hence, contacts and discussions with Beijing should be expanded and regularized to the greatest extent

possible, leading to a strategic dialogue with Beijing that serves to lessen the potential for miscalculation arising from the ongoing Taiwanese democratic process.

ACKNOWLEDGMENTS

This report grew out of work done during the first of two stints as a RAND summer intern. The program brings Ph.D. candidates from a variety of disciplines to RAND to work on various projects, and I am grateful to Glenn Gotz and Jonathan Pollack for hiring me and for giving me the opportunity to pursue this line of inquiry.

At RAND, I am especially grateful to Michael Swaine, who not only supervised the project, but continually pushed and argued with me, sharpened the analysis, and took the decision to bring the report out as a free-standing monograph. Kirsten Speidel lent crucial analytical and administrative support. Her experience with Taiwan is greater and longer than mine, and the insight that experience has given her helped to shape my own thinking about the place. She also helped to negotiate the administrative pitfalls of research and publication, and I am enormously indebted to her because of it.

Ralph Clough read the manuscript in draft and proved a very helpful reviewer. The reader will notice that several of his comments have been incorporated in an explicit way, and the final product owes much to his critique.

Patricia Bedrosian shepherded the manuscript through the RAND publication process, and, as my editor, put up with my stubborn defense of each word in the original draft.

I am grateful to my interviewees in Taiwan and the United States.

Finally, the comments of participants in seminars on Taiwan that I gave at RAND and at the Stanford Center for International Security and Arms Control helped me to settle my own somewhat turbulent thinking at crucial junctures.

ACRONYMS

APEC	Asia-Pacific Economic Cooperation forum
ASEAN	Association of Southeast Asian Nations
CCP	Chinese Communist Party
DPP	Democratic Progressive Party
GATT	General Agreement on Tariffs and Trade
IGO	Inter-Governmental Organization
IMF	International Monetary Fund
KMT	Kuomintang (Taiwan's Nationalist Party)
MFN	Most-Favored Nation
OEM	Original Equipment Manufacturer
PLA	People's Liberation Army
PRC	People's Republic of China
ROC	Republic of China
UN	United Nations
WTO	World Trade Organization

Chapter One

INTRODUCTION

For more than forty years the China-Taiwan conflict has effectively institutionalized the outcome of China's 1945–49 civil war. Since 1949, each side of the Taiwan Strait has been ruled by one of the two main parties to that conflict. Until the late 1980s, the generation of leaders who presided over the division managed the cross-Strait dispute. Moreover, the rhetoric that has defined the Strait conflict— China's refusal to renounce the potential use of force to "finish the job" of national unification, and Taiwan's official claim to be the legitimate government of all China—sets constraints that limited flexibility on both sides, and that rendered real movement in the relationship virtually impossible.

Broadly speaking, these constraints continue to bound the relationship. But since the mid-1980s, the Taiwan authorities have taken a series of decisive steps to open the island's political system to competition and competing views. Local political debate has become exceedingly contentious, and China policy and the island's future status lie at the heart of this freewheeling debate. An opposition party explicitly committed to the goal of Taiwan independence has emerged to challenge the ruling Kuomintang (KMT) at both the national and local levels. The KMT itself has been transformed as the civil war generation gives way to younger, Taiwan-born leaders with a Taiwan-centered political consciousness and no first-hand memory of the mainland. At the same time, Taiwan's business community has invested considerable resources in mainland ventures as restrictions to such investment have gradually been peeled away. While the political debate thus opens an arena for divisive sentiments, economic realities and constraints are driving the two sides together and increasing the interdependence of the two economies.

These extraordinary changes have wiped out many old assumptions. It may no longer be taken for granted, for instance, that the goal of eventual reunification underlies Taiwan's China policy, or its approach to foreign and security affairs. A number of the issues that Beijing explicitly regards as potential conflict triggers are openly discussed on the island. The pro-independence Democratic Progressive Party (DPP) has made gains at the national level since its legalization in 1986. The rise of the DPP has been accompanied by the emergence of independence and the localization of political authority as legitimate topics of public discourse. And despite Beijing's sabre rattling, Taiwan's political evolution along a number of key dimensions continues in ways that cannot be pleasing to China's leadership.

For these reasons, an appreciation of domestic changes in Taiwan, and the ways in which these have altered the Taiwan side's view of the relationship, the reunification issue, and Taiwan's long-term status, is essential. Not only do local political constraints shape Taiwan's policies and constrain the state and the major parties; local political constraints also inject the Taiwan electorate into the dispute. With public opinion bulking so large in Taiwan's domestic politics, it is difficult to imagine a scenario for *peaceful* settlement of the dispute that circumscribes the local political process. So long as public opinion shapes Taiwan's democracy, local trends will push and pull the Taiwan side's policy in ways that alternately infuriate, please, or have no effect on Beijing.

This report therefore places the potential for cross-Strait conflict primarily in the context of domestic change in Taiwan. In the political-military, socio-political, and economic arenas, the report aggregates a variety of domestic trends into six summary conclusions about what underlies and shapes Taiwan's approach to China policy and to foreign and security affairs: three political-military, two socio-political, and one economic. These conclusions reflect the dominant trends and features associated with rapid change in areas as disparate as the institutional character of Taiwan's political system, generational change and the shifting ethnic composition of Taiwan's elite, the breakdown of the ruling party, accelerating offshore investment, continuing economic integration with the mainland, and the connections between economic activity abroad and foreign policy formulation at home. By aggregating disparate trends into general conclusions, the report seeks to organize into a coherent framework the extraordinary change that has taken place in recent years along virtually every dimension of Taiwan's political, economic, and social life. Many of these changes have the potential to destabilize a China-Taiwan relationship already in flux as the civil war generation passes from the scene on both sides of the divide. At the same time, some conclusions reflect trends that may stabilize the relationship, such as the acceleration of investment and increasing economic interdependence. All of these issues have significant implications for the way in which interests are calculated, policy options weighed and chosen, and precisely whose interests are given primacy in Taiwan's policy debate: the state's, those of the parties, of the business community, or those of emergent social and political movements. The aggregation of trends into broad summary conclusions should thus render more clear the demarcation between stabilizing and destabilizing trends. At the end of the report, these conclusions are filtered through three scenarios so as to assess ways in which stabilizing and destabilizing trends crosscut and constrain each other in the process of policy formulation, as well as the concrete implications of these factors for Taiwan's foreign and security behavior. In this way, the scenarios seek to tie potentially contradictory trends together, and to assess ways in which these might trigger adversity in the cross-Strait relationship.

Broadly speaking, the dominant trends and features evident in three arenas will have the greatest effect on Taiwan's approach to China policy; in each arena, these can be aggregated into a series of broad summary conclusions:

- In the political-military arena: the apparent emergence of broad consensus in favor of Taiwan's de facto, though not necessarily de jure, independence; the ruling KMT's effort to accommodate itself to the local constraints associated with this consensus; and the institutional and electoral checks that prevent any party from upsetting this status quo without first forging broad-based, islandwide support for change.

- In the socio-political arena: the pluralization of Taiwan society into interests that share an increasing confidence in Taiwan's capacity to leverage wealth for political gain, but that hold divergent views as to how this might best be accomplished.

- In the economic arena: an ongoing attempt to restructure Taiwan's economy in the direction of capital- and technology-intensive, as opposed to labor-intensive, industry such that the island's dependence on offshore production—and especially on mainland investment—need not be coupled with vulnerability to the political whims of offshore partners.

The analysis that follows argues for short- to medium-term continuity, with the possibility of conflict in the relationship over the longer term. Three conclusions reflect trends that are potentially destabilizing: the political and social changes associated with emerging consensus in favor of Taiwan's "distinct" identity; "Taiwanization" of the ruling KMT; and increasing confidence in Taiwan's capacity to leverage wealth, investment, and trade for ambitious foreign policy goals. These conclusions reflect trends that appear to be pulling Taiwan away from any substantive commitment to reunification. However, three additional conclusions reflect stabilizing trends: constraints on bold policy shifts imposed by Taiwan's electoral system; the emergence of plural, and potentially conflicting, local interests; and continuing economic integration with the mainland. Coupled with security and deterrence issues, these stabilizing trends suggest four structural constraints on Taiwan's foreign and security policy process:

- The Chinese threat and the imperatives of effective deterrence
- The need to forge wide consensus to effect a major shift in China policy
- The diversity of interests complicating the coalition and consensus-building process
- Taiwan's continuing trade dependence, and the rapid expansion of offshore investment.

Taken together, these constraints exert powerful pressure on *all* parties in Taiwan not to upset the delicate balance in the cross-Strait relationship. Over the longer term, however, China's own policy toward Taiwan remains something of a wild card. Furthermore, local worries about long-term economic dependence and more complete economic integration may intertwine with such destabilizing trends as the emerging consensus in favor of a distinct Taiwan identity. Such trends could push independence advocates to view their window of opportunity as closing so long as the present integratory trends persist. In the short to medium term, the four constraints above will likely preclude rash moves by the Taiwan side. These longer-term fears are palpable, however, and the stakes for independence advocates will continue to rise as the process of economic and social integration with the mainland continues apace. In this respect, the tone of the local debate over economic integration and political independence will surely be ratcheted up over time. Such a development cannot but have destabilizing effects on the relationship, none more so than on the potential Chinese response to more intense local discussion of these issues.

Chapter Two

POLITICAL-MILITARY TRENDS: CONSENSUS, THE KMT, AND POLICY INCREMENTALISM

The diverse political-military trends that drive and constrain Taiwan's policy process may be aggregated into three summary conclusions; each is briefly stated below and then elaborated in greater detail at the end of each section:

An Emerging Consensus: Broad consensus appears to have emerged in Taiwan that the current status quo—the island's de facto independence—is the baseline condition for a debate about Taiwan's status.

A New KMT: The ruling KMT is today a different party from the one that managed the Strait conflict from 1949 to approximately 1990. While the KMT will not explicitly back independence, its new leaders clearly consider Taiwan's identity to be distinct from that of the mainland.

Elections, Incrementalism, and Consensus Building: The electoral system in Taiwan places substantive checks on a government's ability to attempt bold policy shifts.

AN EMERGING CONSENSUS

Broad consensus appears to have emerged in Taiwan that the extant status quo—the island's de facto independence—is the minimum acceptable condition for a debate over Taiwan's status. In spite of differences within, and between, the major parties on the status issue—as well as the existence of old guard political views at the margin—nearly all politicians of significance agree that local control over Taiwan's affairs—including commercial, military, political, and exchange relations—is essential to Taiwan's security and to the island's continued viability as an entity distinct from the behemoth of the Chinese mainland. Taiwan has now enjoyed some forty-five years of de facto independence, and the *substance* of that independence is generally regarded as non-negotiable because few Taiwan citizens have experience with the mainland in the context of a unitary polity. Contemporary Taiwan's "Chineseness," much less its local identity, has evolved in a vacuum largely disconnected from direct mainland interference. It is thus a subject of contentious local debate, and leads many on the island to worry about the possibility of Taiwan drowning in a sea of less prosperous, but larger and more politically powerful, Chinese provinces.

In large measure, this consensus has emerged out of the twin phenomena of generational transition and the localization of elite composition, important long-term trends that reflect significant social transformation.

Generational Transition

In its largest sense, generational change has effectively removed from Taiwan's political scene those actors who created the extant status quo and who guided its development for more than forty years. Generational change translates in practice into a leadership with no experience of their island *except* as a de facto independent entity. During the period of these politicians' rise to influence, Taiwan has been self-governed—at lower and middle administrative levels, largely by these very KMT politicians and bureaucrats—has conducted its own trade, structured its own domestic system, and with respect to KMT-opposition interaction, wrestled with its own domestic problems for nearly half a century. These developments have evolved against the backdrop of little direct interference from the mainland. And this weak mainland frame of reference, together with the ruling and opposition party leaderships' rise to prominence in a Taiwan-specific electoral setting, is a genuine shift from the experience of the generation that governed Taiwan from 1945 to approximately 1990.

Generational change, moreover, means that for most of Taiwan's present (and future) leaders, old orthodoxies are largely inherited rather than based upon first-hand experience. Anti-communism, in the absence of direct experience of combat with the Chinese communists, cannot but become an abstract; "One China" claims ring increasingly hollow in the absence of a mainland-specific frame of political reference. Taiwan's "China problem" is thus increasingly conceptualized in security and deterrence, as opposed to political-ideological, terms. Finally, generational change means that most contemporary Taiwan citizens have no direct experience of the mainland except as tourists or visitors, and this includes nominal "mainlanders" in the Taiwan populace (see Figure 2.1). A 1987 survey suggested that no more than 5 percent of the census population *at that time* had been born on the mainland prior to 1950.[1] That

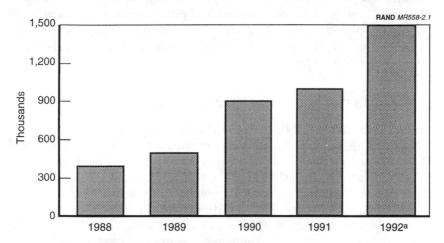

RAND MR558-2.1

aFirst seven months at annual rate.
SOURCE: China Travel Service.
Reprinted by permission from: *The Economist*, October 10, 1992.

Figure 2.1—Taiwanese Visits to Mainland China

---

[1] *Tianxia* [*Commonwealth*, Taipei], No. 70, March 1, 1987. Cited in Tien (1992), fn 31, p. 54. NOTE: Pinyin romanization is used in the present document for terms in Chinese, with the exception of the following, which use the Wade-Giles system: names such as Chiang Kai-shek, Sun Yat-sen, Taipei, and Kuomintang and names of individuals living outside mainland China.

number is no doubt smaller today, and experience with the mainland in any role save that of visitor is thus increasingly rare in Taiwan.

This dwindling of the number of genuine "mainlanders" raises questions about primary identities and about the extent to which localism has developed population-wide. To the extent that China is equated with a place that is "visited" as opposed to "lived in," local identification becomes a salient part of the average Taiwan citizen's *political* identity. Thus, while increased contact and visitation are no doubt changing where and how China fits into the Taiwanese frame of reference and are important counterpoints to this trend—and Beijing relies upon these to counter Taiwan's drift—they cannot alter the fact of primary identification with Taiwan. On the purely anecdotal level this is reflected in the comments of visitors returning from the mainland. More significantly, it is reflected in local campaign style: Even second-generation "mainlander" politicians often campaign in dialect, while ethnically Taiwanese KMT candidates have at times endeavored to play the "ethnic card" against fellow partisans of mainland extraction.[2]

Localization of Elite Composition

When generational shift is coupled with the phenomenon of localization of elite composition, the disconnection between Taiwan and China takes on specifically political significance. Localization—or "Taiwanization"—has shattered the ethnic division of labor that preserved mainlander dominance in party, state, judicial, and military and police institutions. Most politicians and bureaucrats on the island are now locals: in 1992 some 80 percent of KMT legislative candidates were ethnically Taiwanese, as opposed to merely Taiwan-born. This figure reached 98 percent for the DPP, and as high as 89 percent for independent and minor party candidates.[3] Moreover, Taiwan's KMT president and premier are also ethnically Taiwanese.

In strategic terms, this transformation is (potentially) destabilizing when set against the backdrop of the reunification issue. For more

---

[2]*Far Eastern Economic Review (FEER)*, November 19, 1992, p. 22; *FEER*, November 12, 1992, p. 20.

[3]*FEER*, October 1, 1992, p. 14.

than a generation, mainlander hegemony in Taiwan's political institutions went hand-in-hand with the island's continued insistence on the "One China" claim. Since the KMT's claim to legitimacy rested in China, not Taiwan, and since it lacked a specifically local electoral mandate to rule the island at the national level until the early 1990s, an exiled administration resident in Taiwan *province* (in the context of a continuing *national* civil war) was the only basis upon which to legitimately ground an uncompromising, ethnically based authoritarian political system. Elite patriotism aside, the KMT relied on its claim to mainland sovereignty as a means to simultaneously claim legitimacy for its rule of Taiwan by martial law and emergency decree. The claim to China and the heavy hand of the party-state in large measure evolved in tandem.

But with democratization, and the "Taiwanization" of an ever-increasing share of the KMT and state leadership, ethnicity has been rendered less salient as a political criterion. Much of the opposition's early appeal was based upon the not unfair perception that the KMT was a "mainlander" party with primary commitment across the Strait rather than to Taiwan, and the KMT's unrelenting talk about China and the China claim no doubt reinforced this. The emergence of what amounts in practice to a Taiwanese KMT effectively localizes the political debate and steals opposition thunder. Democracy and localization of the elite raise questions about the commitment of Taiwan's KMT elite to reunification and to the mainland. Such issues of commitment were once confined to Taiwan's masses and to non-KMT elites. A mainlander KMT, after all, remained strongly committed to its "One China" rhetoric because the party-state, and a party-penetrated military establishment, continued to regard the mainland as its political center of gravity. But a "Taiwanized" party-state, bureaucracy, and—increasingly—military raise questions about the extent to which Taiwan's elites continue to believe their own "One China" and reunification rhetoric. With the Taiwan state open at all levels to locals, and the legislature populated by ethnically Taiwanese politicians, much less Taiwan-born "mainlanders," the KMT may be hard pressed to sustain the legal fiction of the "Republic of China" should it confront sustained opposition and independence sentiment at home. Indeed, given localization, it may no longer wish to, except for purposes of deterring the Chinese threat.

There thus exists a mutually conditioning relationship between Taiwanization, the formation of a thoroughly local identity, and the long-term relationship between the two sides of the Strait. Localization, together with generational shift, no doubt weakens the Taiwan side's commitment to its official rhetoric, irrespective of which coalition or party holds power: there is little ethnic basis for it given the shifting location of primary personal and collective identification; there is certainly less generational basis for it, and that is a trend that can only be exacerbated by the passing of what remains of the KMT old guard.

Conclusion 1

Underpinned by generational transition and the localization of Taiwan's elite, broad consensus appears to have emerged that the current status quo—Taiwan's de facto independence—is the baseline condition for a debate about the island's status. While the opposition DPP expresses preference for eventual de jure independence, and divisions exist within the KMT on the status issue, virtually none among the key political figures on the island, much less public opinion, would voluntarily accept a solution that trades away Taiwan's authority over each of the areas in which it presently exercises de facto independence. By this logic, barring significant compromise, no peaceful settlement of the Taiwan issue can leave the island with less authority *in practice* than it currently exercises over its own affairs.[4]

---

[4]From the Taiwan side, such compromise could include acceptance of "unequal" status with Beijing in the cross-Strait dialogue or abandonment of the principles of genuine autonomy. Taiwan has not declared independence, for instance, but Lee Teng-hui has declared that "the Republic of China on Taiwan is a sovereign country" (May 20, 1993, press conference). Were Taiwan to bargain over aspects of the meaning of local "sovereignty," making concessions in any cross-Strait dialogue to *Beijing's* interpretation of this term, this would, in my view, represent a compromise on Taipei's part. Beijing's interpretation, after all, tends more toward the equation of "sovereignty" with "autonomy" whereas Lee's version surely leans in the direction of de facto independence. With respect to Beijing's stance, acceptance of the "Taiwan authorities" as an "equal" dialogue partner would represent a significant shift in Chinese policy.

A NEW KMT

These patterns of localization and generational transition have drastically affected leadership and legitimacy within the ruling KMT. They have altered the composition of the party's leadership, and, by extension, the manner in which party policy on the status issue has evolved over time.

Lee Teng-hui is the first ethnically Taiwanese politician to occupy the presidency, and his rise to Taiwan's highest office ushered in an era of comparatively rapid turnover in which the highest ranks of the KMT, and many of Taiwan's highest offices, have been filled by others of Taiwanese extraction; these include Lien Chan, the incumbent premier. In fact, the decision to bring ethnic Taiwanese into the highest reaches of party and government was a conscious one. As early as the 1960s, the KMT moved to bolster legitimacy by coopting local elites into the ranks of the island's political elite. Perhaps inevitably, this process accelerated as a function of numbers. But Lee's rise to the top has had profound implications for the party. For the first time, the two leading offices on the island—the presidency and the premiership—are occupied by locally born politicians. Moreover, as noted above, some 80 percent of KMT candidates in the 1992 Legislative Yuan poll were of ethnic Taiwanese extraction, as opposed to merely Taiwan-born. The KMT, not unlike its DPP rival, which once played up the ethnic cleavage between the two parties, has itself emerged as a Taiwanese party.

This transformation of its ethnic composition has formed the backdrop to a series of internal convulsions that have begun to significantly change the KMT and its approach to mainland policy. A first set of trends revolves about the triumph of Lee's "Taiwanese moderates" over old guard elites, as well as second-generation mainlanders who ultimately defected from the party. A second trend is tied to the party's increasingly flexible approach to the status issue, and a third set of trends concerns the changing relationship between the KMT and Taiwan's armed forces and security services.

The Evolving KMT "Center"

Though the KMT has yet to emerge from recent convulsions as a thoroughly coherent party, a somewhat loose group, clustered about Lee, has nonetheless succeeded in marginalizing two alternative sets of KMT leaders: old guard elites, who have retired, died, or been marginalized by the pace of events, and popular second-generation mainlanders, who defected from the KMT to form the New Party. Three specific events of the past three years capture the nature of this evolution. Though the first two initially raised questions about Lee's leadership, they seem in retrospect to have strengthened his hand.

*   *Marginalizing the Old Guard:* Lee's 1990 election to the presidency in his own right required that he face down a near-rebellion from within the KMT. Because Vice President Lee's "accidental" succession upon Chiang Ching-kuo's death was viewed by many old guard elites as transitional, his move to strengthen his authority and subsequent quest for reelection to the presidency alienated a number of older elites, including then Premier Lee Huan and other powerful mainlanders on the KMT Central Committee. A rebel faction, nominally led by a Taiwanese, Lin Yang-kang, but backed by a number of senior party figures including Lin's ostensible "running-mate" Chiang Wei-kuo,[5] threatened to challenge Lee for the party nomination, and Lee's ultimate triumph was thus won at a price: an informal "committee" of party elders was asked to persuade Lin and Chiang to withdraw, raising a variety of questions about the strength of Lee's leadership.[6] But the 1990 election was in some sense the old guard's last hurrah. For with mainland-elected legislators forcibly retired by court order, the KMT won a re-sounding victory in the first formal test of Lee's leadership, the 1991 National Assembly poll, by posting younger, generally Taiwanese, candidates and staking out a less provocative approach to the status issue than the DPP's. Moreover, Lee skillfully turned a subsequent "defeat"—the DPP's capture of approximately a third of the popular vote in the 1992 Legislative

---

[5]Chiang Kai-shek's son, Chiang Ching-kuo's half-brother, and director of the powerful National Security Council.

[6]Background and greater detail is provided in Ts'ai and Myers (1992).

Yuan poll (see Table 2.1)—into an unexpected opportunity to dismiss a remaining rallying point of the mainlander old guard, the mainland-born general-turned-premier, Hau Po-ts'un. Though Lin Yang-kang is frequently mentioned as a candidate should Lee not seek reelection—and Lee's intentions remain unclear—it is important to remember that Lin, too, is ethnically Taiwanese, and would no doubt face stiff opposition from politicians more closely associated with the president, such as Premier Lien Chan.

- *Second-Generation Defection:* The defection of second-genera-tion mainlander politicians again raised questions about Lee's leadership but in effect removed another key group of the presi-dent's critics from KMT ranks. Most analysts in Taiwan suggest that the New Party will siphon electoral support from the KMT; its second-generation mainlander leadership is widely popular and draws off a natural base of support in certain KMT con-stituencies as well as populist appeals. But with nearly all of the KMT's heaviest hitters now ethnically Taiwanese, and at least loosely grouped about Lee Teng-hui, an opportunity exists for

Table 2.1

Net Results of 1992 Legislative Yuan Election

Party	No. of Candi-dates	Votes Received	Total Votes (%)	District Seats Won	At Large Seats National/ Overseas
KMT					
Nominees	125	5,031,259	53.0	73	27/6
Non-nominees	43	710,203	7.5	7	0
Total KMT	168	5,741,462	60.5	80	19/4
DPP					
Nominees	59	2,944,195	31.0	37	16/3
Non-nominees	8	78,638	0.8	0	0
Total DPP	67	3,022,833	31.9	37	11/2
CSDP[a]	22	126,213	1.3	1	0
Other parties	20	56,083	0.6	0	0
Independents	71	542,714	5.7	7	0
Total	348	9,489,305	100.0	125	30/6

[a]Chinese Social Democratic Party.

Source: *China Post* (Taipei), 21 December 1992, p. 16.

Reprinted from *China Quarterly*, No. 136, December 1993, p. 822.

the party to reconstitute itself by remaking its image before the electorate. The "old" KMT, which the DPP stridently attacked as a mainlander preserve, is a rhetorical anachronism. And with the New Party defections, what remains of the KMT is a predominantly Taiwanese party with a new policy look—flexible on China policy and diplomatic issues—but with many of the electoral and financial levers of the old party machine still at its disposal.

• *Strengthening Lee's Hand:* Lee's active—and arguably decisive— role in promoting KMT candidates at the 1993 local polls should put to rest for the moment questions about his leadership, and about the "new" KMT's ability to compete. A confident DPP leadership had predicted victory in as many as 50 percent of local races. In the event, Lee broke with tradition and campaigned hard for KMT candidates, personally visiting local constituencies and participating in KMT-sponsored campaign events. The KMT's surprisingly good showing leads to four conclusions about Lee and the new KMT:

  – Lee's intervention appears to have made the difference in many races; active presidential intervention was unprecedented in Taiwan, and the president's hand was strengthened as a result of KMT victories.

  – The 1991 and 1992 national polls, and the 1993 local elections, though for different levels of government, produced results reflecting voter swing to one or the other major party; the December 1994 poll, Taiwan's most recent, yielded split results for the island's two most important local offices, with the KMT retaining the provincial governorship, and the DPP capturing the Taipei mayoralty. A relatively stable two-party system, with the New Party as wild card, appears to be developing.

  – Local machines and candidate personality matter a great deal in electoral contests; cliché party labels—the KMT as "mainlander preserve," the DPP as "radical provocateur"— appear to mean little to the voters.

  – Issue-based campaigns are bound to become more important; with constitutional and ethnic disputes no longer truly relevant, "real" public policy stands—including stands on the status issue—will define the difference between parties and their candidates.

Indeed, the KMT's success at the 1993 local polls was followed by continuing success in January 1994 mayoral and city council contests and retention of the Taiwan governorship in December 1994. At the January polls, though tarnished by record incidents of electoral violence, the KMT captured as many as 82 percent of the 858 contestable council seats, and 309 city and township mayoralties. The party's showing puts to rest for the moment questions about its ability to compete. In the run-up to Taiwan's first direct presidential election, however, the party may need to begin the search for a successor to Lee Teng-hui. Reports suggest the president's disinclination to run for another term, but Lee remains enormously popular, his intentions murky, and the KMT exceedingly sluggish on the succession issue. In part, this reflects Lee's popularity and the hope among many party faithful that he can be drafted to run in 1996; yet it also reflects the lack of an alternative candidate likely to prove viable in the face of strong DPP opposition. Though Lin Yang-kang has already declared himself a candidate, he lacks Lee's popularity, as do other probable contenders, such as Lien Chan. This, together with the comparatively good showing independent candidates made in the 1994 city polls, confronts the KMT with important questions of strategy.

Perhaps inevitably, these changes in the ethnic composition of the leadership and rank and file, as well as in the KMT's policy positions, have begun to affect the party's approach to mainland policy. As the old approach—rigid insistence on the "One China" and Republic of China claims—has become anachronistic, the KMT has staked out ground meant to display flexibility yet at the same time to distinguish its approach from that of the "radical" DPP opposition.

Official Claims and Policy Flexibility

A second trend reflecting the evolution of a new KMT concerns the party's gradual retreat from its old claims in practice while simultaneously attempting to preserve the official version of the claim for deterrence purposes. Thus while Taiwan remains the Republic of China, and reunification a subject of official discourse, KMT leaders have adjusted to local political constraints by staking out middle ground between the DPP's independence approach and the "old" KMT's reunification approach. In part, this is in response to the substantial popular pressure in Taiwan to boost the island's international standing: the disjuncture between Taiwan's economic and diplomatic weight in the world is a subject of contentious local debate. But although the KMT is vulnerable on this issue and has sought to be more flexible on the matter of Taiwan's status, it walks a fine line between public pressures on the one hand, and adequate deterrence on the other. Some positions are still regarded as too "radical": In late 1992 the party expelled a legislator who had expressed support for the DPP's "One China, One Taiwan" formula.[7] Yet it is significant that the KMT's stand continues to evolve, and that officials as prominent as Premier Lien Chan have insisted that Taiwan receive United Nations representation. Within the KMT, a combination of popular political pressure and, perhaps, the inclinations of an ethnically Taiwanese leadership are dragging the party away from its old claims and into a middle ground between the DPP and the old approach. This crosscuts issues raised in the section on "Flexibility and Confidence" (Conclusion 4) and will be considered in greater detail below.

Demilitarized Politics, Depoliticization of the Military

Finally, in a third set of trends, the intimate relationship between the KMT and Taiwan's armed forces and security services has come under attack from the opposition and from social groups. In the context of the old party-state regime, such attacks meant little. But in the new democracy, with the opposition gaining strength at the national level, the issue of party-army coordination has political ramifications. Gradually, the military's domestic functions have been peeled away, and many of its roles and missions parceled out to agencies within the larger state bureaucracy. Simultaneously, discussion of the means to institutionalize state, as opposed to party-based, checks in the civil-military sphere has become more salient. The result of both trends is a marked decline in the military's importance as a domestic actor; its role in foreign policy, and especially

---

[7] *FEER*, December 24, 1992, p. 25.

policymaking regarding China, however, remains considerably more ambiguous.

- *Abolished Institutions and the Pattern of Military Influence:* Under the state of civil war that prevailed until martial law was lifted in 1987, the military played a formidable role in Taiwan's domestic affairs. Under emergency rule, a variety of institutions designed to regulate dissent were established, and Taiwan's military took on domestic police and surveillance functions, in addition to its role in coastal defense and customs surveillance. With the removal of the state of emergency, the government automatically terminated the mandate meant to legitimate institutions such as the feared Garrison Command. Established by presidential decree in 1958, the Command was widely accused of torture and cast a wide net in the lives of Taiwan citizens for more than twenty years. By terminating the Command's mandate and parceling its surveillance and censorship functions out to the National Police Administration, the Ministry of Justice, and the Government Information Office, the government removed one of the most powerful symbols of the old regime. More generally, the state accelerated the process of demilitarizing national political life. Though many in the opposition continue to raise questions about the degree to which old activities persist under new supervision, the termination of the *legal* basis for such activities effectively undercut the military's role in domestic politics. Tight party-army coordination has long been the norm in Taiwan's Leninist-style political structure. To begin the process of institutionalizing state-based checks on the armed forces, termination of the military's domestic activities was therefore vital. While the military has traditionally been less powerful as an institution than via its connections to the Chiang family and the party, these wide-ranging domestic roles lent it an institutional weight in the everyday lives of Taiwan citizens, which belied its status as a policy institution in the decisionmaking structure at the apex. The general demilitarization of political life has thus undoubtedly eroded the military's broad policy role even as it allows the state to fashion a more institutionalized, narrow, and regularized role for the armed forces in the evolving policymaking structure of the new regime.

- *Depoliticization and the Broadened Security Debate:* Significantly, this trend has been accompanied, and reinforced, by broadened debate of military issues outside the immediate context of the Executive Yuan. The legislature boasts the most significant opposition presence among national-level political institutions. And as the new Legislative Yuan's recent budget debates witnessed the first serious attempt by the chamber to narrow the government's proposals for military expenditures and foreign arms purchases, there are indications that oversight and military issues will be important to watch on two levels.

    – First, the development of regularized *state,* as opposed to party, oversight over the military, together with the battle among government branches for the upper hand in this struggle for control, will no doubt occupy an increasingly prominent place in the domestic debate. The KMT long employed a commissar system to control the military, laying great stress on Leninist-type party-military coordination.[8] While the military has often been active in Taiwan politics, it has thus been active less as an institution than as a set of interests within the broader structure of the KMT party-state. But the evolution of Taiwan's political system has not been accompanied by the total replacement of *party-based* civilian checks with strong, regularized, and institutionalized checks anchored in the state structure. Thus the DPP can be expected to push for a forced erosion of KMT-military ties. Yet the oversight issue is compounded by the fact that military leaders have long been assumed to lie *politically* within the conservative mainlander camp of the KMT. Hau Po-ts'un, Lien Chan's predecessor as premier, served as defense minister and armed forces commander prior to his move to the top of the Executive Yuan. And the likely persistence of an ethnic division of labor at the *highest* levels of the military, when compared with the situation in other key institutions of the polity—with senior officers still of predominantly mainlander extraction (though this division has probably waned among more junior colleagues) and enlisted men almost entirely of Taiwanese background—complicates the effort to

---

[8]For background, see Cheng (1990), pp. 123–144.

impose state-based, party-blind, and *politically neutral* controls on Taiwan's armed forces.

- Second, the place that military and security issues occupy in the debate between parties continues to evolve. Military issues have long been a KMT domain, and the level of security expertise in the DPP appears comparatively low.[9] Yet as the political stakes are raised, and as the DPP becomes a serious contender for power, China policy and independence debates continue to heat up. And security questions—Taiwan's capacity to deter a PRC attack—inevitably bring the political context of the debate around to military issues, weapons purchases, tough budget decisions, and international security commitments. Indeed, Taiwan has drastically increased the pace and scale of its purchases in the past two years. Hau's defense minister Ch'en Li'an points out that "from the 1960s through the 1980s, Taiwan lacked the resources to purchase weaponry; in the 1980s, although Taiwan had the resources to do so, it nonetheless failed to purchase the weapons it needed."[10] In the 1990s, Taiwan has actively sought to purchase weapons from abroad, and should be expected to actively push for continuing access to high technology weapons systems—with a focus on air and naval technologies—but at a somewhat reduced pace as budget pressures kick in. China's aggressive moves to purchase ad-

---

[9]There are exceptions, of course, such as Ch'en Shui-pien. But a continuing problem for the DPP is that legislators such as Ch'en, who have made names for themselves in foreign and defense debates before the Legislative Yuan, may become attractive as contenders for executive positions without foreign and defense responsibility. This is precisely what happened to Ch'en Shui-pien, whose election as Taipei mayor in December 1994 was an important victory for the DPP, but one that removed an important party spokesman from security debates in the legislature. I am indebted to Ralph Clough for pointing out to me Ch'en's legislative work in the security arena (personal communication, October 26, 1994).

[10]"Taiwan junhuo cong nali lai?" [Where does Taiwan's weaponry come from?], *Jiushi niandai* [*The Nineties*, Hong Kong], May 1991, p. 54. On air priorities, see Fic (1993). On naval needs, see *FEER*, February 4, 1993, pp. 10–11. For a comprehensive discussion of military needs and weapons purchases through 1991, see "Haixia liang'an de junhuo maimai: zhuanti" [The weapons trade on the two sides of the Strait: A Special Report], *Jiushi niandai* [*The Nineties*, Hong Kong], May 1991, pp. 51–63. For a comparative discussion of Chinese and Taiwan capabilities, tactics, and strategy, see Godwin (1993).

vanced weaponry have convinced many policymakers in Taipei that the imperatives of effective deterrence compel the island to employ what leverage it has in the interests of security and military needs. In the event, Taiwan will certainly employ economic leverage, and dangle the prospect of new sales before U.S. and European contractors, to attract sale permissions in higher technology areas. As Ch'en's comment makes clear, there is a widespread perception in Taiwan defense circles that the island squandered past opportunities to purchase advanced systems, and that similar mistakes must not be made now that Beijing appears intent on upgrading the People's Liberation Army's (PLA's) weaponry and its shopping list consists primarily of the kind of conventional air and naval systems likely to see action in the Strait. This inevitably sharpens the domestic debate as the military's wants and needs eat up a considerable portion of the budget; many legislators view such spending as excessive. In light of the Chinese threat of force, any reduction in military expenditures must inevitably filter back through the *political* debate about threats from China and the proper way to manage China policy and the issue of Taiwan's status. Though budgeting and manpower issues have heretofore played a comparatively small role in the partisan domestic debate, they are likely to occupy an increasingly prominent place in Taiwan as the stakes of the China policy and independence debates similarly increase. Taiwan is committed to paying for the F-16s it was permitted by the Bush Administration to purchase in 1992. These are scheduled to begin arriving on the island in 1996, and Taiwan must also pay for the French Mirage fighters it ordered at approximately the same time, as well as for frigates and additional naval craft. Preoccupied with training and maintenance, the Taiwan Air Force seems unlikely to push for new purchases in the immediate term, but the tension between budget outlays, wider demands on government resources, and the continuing need to provide a credible deterrent to China's military power remains.

Conclusion 2

The ruling KMT is a different party from the one that managed the Strait conflict from 1949 to approximately 1990. While the party's center of gravity once lay on the mainland, and the KMT was regarded by many locals in Taiwan as a "mainlander" institution, the rise of younger, locally born party leaders and the need to compete in a Taiwan-specific electoral setting have opened once unquestioned orthodoxies to internal scrutiny. Internal discussions of the status issue no longer assume that a "One China" solution is the *only* possible basis for a resolution of the conflict. Rather, "One China, Two Governments," and a variety of proposals that smack of "Two Chinas" or "One China, One Taiwan" scenarios are openly discussed or only halfheartedly muzzled. In this context, the sigh of relief with which Beijing once greeted KMT victories over the DPP may no longer be justified. While the KMT will not explicitly back independence, its new leaders clearly consider Taiwan's identity to be distinct, hence their demand that the island be admitted to United Nations (UN) membership. While the mere fact of the KMT's existence once provided an apparent check on independence sentiment, the party's approach to the status issue no longer mirrors Beijing's in the absolute. Unlike Hong Kong, where the constituency for Beijing's views appears both large and deep, in Taiwan the constituency for the old approach has been increasingly marginalized by the process of political change. Furthermore, long-standing links between the KMT and a party-penetrated military establishment have come in for criticism from Taiwan's opposition. A general demilitarization of political life in Taiwan may, over time, make a more complete depoliticization of the island's military establishment inevitable, especially as the ethnic composition of the officer corps changes. In the process, the KMT's virtual monopoly on security expertise must come to be balanced by greater efforts on the part of DPP and other non-KMT interests to thrust themselves into the heart of the island's security debate.

ELECTIONS, INCREMENTALISM, AND CONSENSUS BUILDING

The electoral system in Taiwan, as well as a yet uncertain balance between state institutions, places substantive checks on a government's ability to attempt bold policy shifts.

Elections and Policy Constraints

At three years, Taiwan's legislative election cycle is relatively short; moreover, elections for a variety of offices have sent voters to the polling booths in each of the past four years, and the addition of direct presidential elections in 1996 will add another poll to those for which voters must already prepare. This structural constraint—the frequency of the election cycle—leaves little room for a government to attempt bold policy shifts. With little lag-time between polls, any government, irrespective of party, faces a referendum on its policies before these have had much time to take effect. After an apparent setback in the 1992 Legislative Yuan poll, for instance, the KMT might have inclined toward a cautious approach to public policy, carefully testing the waters with an eye to upcoming polls. Only one year later, though, the party ran more strongly than expected at the local level, and this apparent vote of confidence, together with continuing victories into 1994, including retention of the Taiwan governorship in a hotly contested December election, has boosted its morale. But with another legislative poll due in 1995—and the loss of the Taipei mayoralty in December to the DPP's popular Ch'en Shui-pien—the KMT faces a very short grace period indeed. Moreover, direct presidential elections are now scheduled for 1996, and other local polls will likely be held during this period. For these reasons, the policy process has become highly politicized; elections often take on the character of referenda, and this has had a number of profound repercussions for the policy process and the political system:

- *Moderate Tendencies:* A 1991 rout by the KMT, followed by a boost for the DPP in 1992, and greater confidence in the KMT at the 1993 and 1994 local polls indicate that Taiwan voters disapprove of radical stands. Though the public mood is decisively on the side of change, it is also for caution with respect to the

Chinese threat. The DPP's comparatively radical stand on independence in 1991 is widely believed to explain its crushing defeat in the 1991 National Assembly poll. When the DPP toned down its more strident rhetoric in 1992, it ran well. In 1993, as DPP leaders predicted the gradual marginalization of the KMT and the DPP's eventual emergence as the island's majority party, the KMT ran better than expected. One must be cautious, of course, about confounding islandwide with local trends: as Joseph Bosco points out, local polls often turn on issues of candidate personality or on issues "closer to the ground" of most Taiwanese citizens' lives. The KMT enjoys enormous advantages in local contests, given an effective islandwide party organization, significant financial resources, and long experience at the manipulation of local factions.[11] In the main, however, decisive—yet ultimately cautious—stands for change seem most likely to win the electorate's votes; most Taiwanese appear to prefer centrist politics. Given the frequency of the election cycle, this sentiment places real checks on the ability of a government of either party to attempt bold policy shifts and then to ride out the storm in the period between polls.

- *The Emerging Political Center:* A "sizable center" appears to be emerging in Taiwan politics, as the DPP is forced to moderate its more radical positions before the voters and the KMT attempts to stand for change without provocation. In comments in the wake of the 1993 local polls, Jaw Shau-kang—the New Party leader—charged that his party represents a voice for genuine change in a system with two parties on their way toward convergence. With respect to electoral politics, Jaw probably overstates his case. With respect to governance, however, Taiwan's largest parties may find that three specific circumstances—the Chinese threat, the need to protect investments on the mainland, and a comparatively cautious electorate—force their policy stands more closely together. *In essence, the policy challenge, though not electoral politics, is blind to partisanship.* The result may be the emergence of a constituency in both parties for cautious advance: the policy dilemma the two parties face is similar; the

---

[11]Bosco (1994). See also chapters on local electoral politics in Cheng and Haggard (1992).

need not to antagonize the electorate—or Beijing—holds constant for both major parties.[12]

The Institutional Balance of State Power

Once in power, all leaders face similar institutional challenges. Newly overhauled, the legislative branch is now the most direct link at the national level between Taiwan voters and their leaders. The new constitution, however, grants the president powers of appointment to three of the five branches of Taiwan's government—the Executive, Judicial, and Control Yuan—and the president, too, will be directly elected in 1996. As a result, struggles between the executive and legislative branches—and the balance of constitutional authority—will prove significant in the evolving polity.

With the Legislative Yuan now the most direct link between Taiwan citizens and state power, its members have proved increasingly willing to test the boundaries of its relationship with the Executive Yuan and the presidency. This is manifest on at least two levels:

* Legislators have vigorously challenged executive officials in committee hearings. Where the KMT could once count on a solid block of friendly sentiment in the chamber, hearings at which ministers and officials have testified have occasionally grown contentious. KMT legislators, too, have joined the fray. Premier Lien Chan's confirmation process, for instance, was unprecedented in the degree to which the nominee was peppered with questions about personal matters such as family finances; much of the most vigorous questioning came from the KMT legislators who later defected to form the New Party.[13]

---

[12]The narrow difference between the two parties in so many areas of public policy translates into widespread dissatisfaction in public opinion surveys. In fact, recent polling data reveal that public concerns have not translated into real support for either party. See "Guomindang gexin: mei xinxin, Minjindang zhizheng: bu fangxin; liangdang jingzheng: minyi diaocha" [No confidence in KMT innovation, unease about the DPP in power; the two-party competition: a survey of popular views], *Tianxia* [*Commonwealth*, Taipei], July 1, 1993, pp. 136–143.

[13]*FEER*, March 4, 1993, p. 12.

- Weak party discipline and a strong orientation toward constituent needs make for autonomous legislators and the periodic emergence of what the daily *Lianhebao* terms "non-partisan voting blocs."[14]   In recent months the government's military budget has been challenged by legislators of both major parties, the Executive has worried about cooperation between opposition and renegade KMT legislators on confirmation votes and, most prominently, legislators cooperated on the so-called "sunshine" legislation designed to expose officials' assets to public scrutiny.[15]   Lien Chan himself—the scion of one of Taiwan's wealthiest families—was a target of pointed questioning on personal finances.[16]

These struggles are particularly significant given the emergence of the DPP as a serious contender for power. With the next president to be directly elected, it is now conceivable that either a split government or a wholly DPP government could emerge. In the former case, the struggle among branches would take on policy significance: could one branch, each controlled by a different party, block the other's initiatives? In the latter, the DPP will undoubtedly face many of the same policy challenges now confronting the KMT. Moreover, the comparative strength of the legislature in the still-evolving political process will dictate a legislative opposition's capacity to resist Executive policy initiatives. Thus a DPP government that pushed for immediate de jure independence might face significant opposition challenges from the KMT and the New Party. Likewise, should the KMT attempt to arrange a party-to-party settlement with the Chinese Communist Party (CCP), without taking other views on the island into account, it would face markedly different opposition from a DPP able to effectively utilize the levers provided the opposition in a strengthened legislature.

---

[14] *Lianhebao* [*United Daily News*, Taipei], June 13, 1993, p. 1.

[15] *Lianhebao,* June 9, 1993.

[16] *FEER,* March 4, 1993.

Conclusion 3

The electoral system in Taiwan places substantive checks on a government's ability to attempt bold policy shifts. Because Taiwan's election cycle is so short—legislative terms are only three years, and the island is currently undergoing a virtual year-to-year election cycle in which national, local, and the first direct presidential elections (now scheduled for 1996) are being held—the policy process has become highly politicized. With parties forced to seek public legitimation so frequently, elections take on the character of referenda. These political realities promote incrementalism in the policy process: a party-to-party deal between the KMT and the Chinese Communists would likely prove unacceptable to voters; a DPP victory and quick declaration of independence might appear unduly provocative. The electoral process thus reinforces the need to forge islandwide consensus on China policy and the independence issue. But while incrementalism may lend stability to the process by checking tendencies to act rashly, it also bogs the process down and may eventually test Beijing's patience. The longer the separation continues, China's leaders may reason, the more likely that Taiwan's separation will become institutionalized. Given the presence of forces undermining "One China" sentiment in Taiwan, Beijing's impatience may precipitate some form of Chinese action.

Chapter Three
SOCIO-POLITICAL TRENDS: FLEXIBLE POLICY, CONFIDENT IDENTITY, AND SOCIAL PLURALIZATION

Socio-political trends that have altered the context of political and policy activity in Taiwan may be aggregated into two summary conclusions:

Flexibility and Confidence: Taiwan is not merely more flexible on issues of status but is increasingly confident in that flexibility. Where Chinese threats once checked independence sentiment, those threats, while palpable, no longer seem so menacing to the island's leadership.

Multiple Interests and Coalition Building: Taiwan has become a more complex place than it was under the civil war generation. Where one interest—the KMT's—once defined the reunification issue, and two interests—the KMT's and the DPP's—eventually supplanted the old approach, multiple interests on the island now have distinct and often conflicting stakes in Taiwan's mainland policy.

FLEXIBILITY AND CONFIDENCE

Taiwan is not merely more flexible on issues of status but is increasingly confident in that flexibility. The government has sought to bring Taiwan's diplomatic and political weight into line with its regional, and even global, economic influence. This policy enjoys virtually universal popular support and is the aspect of Taiwan's foreign and economic policy most likely to antagonize Beijing, particularly if the island attempts to parlay its influence into a larger role in multilateral political or security—as opposed merely to economic—organizations and regimes.

Taiwan's strategy is two-pronged: The island seeks to upgrade its status, and to "internationalize" the Taiwan question by raising its profile in inter-governmental organizations (IGOs) and regimes; at the same time, Taiwan's leaders hope to calm Beijing by stressing continuing engagement via investment, exchange relations, and international support for China's reforms.

Diplomacy and Flexibility on Status Issues

To officials who worry about economic "dependence"—or about Taiwan's marginalization should China successfully sustain high rates of growth and large-scale weapons purchases—raising the island's profile effectively *internationalizes* its status while raising the stakes of a potential conflict with China. The government's heavy emphasis in recent years on participation in international organizations such as the General Agreement on Tariffs and Trade (GATT) and the United Nations is thus in some sense intended as a constraint on potential Chinese action and as a means to institutionalize the status quo—Taiwan's de facto independence from Chinese control—at a minimum. This strategy explicitly intends to give the international community a stake in the extant status quo, and thus in Taiwan's continued viability as an autonomous entity.[1]

The most striking manifestation of the new flexibility is the departure from four decades of unwavering insistence on the letter of the Republic of China and "One China" claims. At the bilateral level, Taiwan no longer demands derecognition of Beijing in exchange for recognition of Taipei. In practice, this amounts to a "Two China" policy, and Beijing has reacted sharply by severing relations with any nation tempted to permit two embassies. From Beijing's vantage point, the presence of two embassies lays the groundwork for Taiwan's eventual independence.

---

[1]A good example of the government's emphasis is Lee Teng-hui's statement at a university commencement that "squeezing Taiwan out" of international organizations is "neither moral nor fair." Taiwan's personality in "international society," Lee argued, is now a fact that cannot be ignored by the global community. *Lianhebao*, June 13, 1993, p. 1.

In multilateral settings, the new flexibility is manifest in Taiwan's willingness to exchange concessions on form for the substance of participation in organizations and regimes. This grants privileges normally accorded "genuine" states and, Taipei reasons, internationalizes the island's status by giving others a stake in any change in the status quo. Taiwan's leaders appear to have concluded that the "One China" claim now undercuts the island's substantive interests. Indeed, as another observer has pointed out, by insisting that the Taiwan issue is internal to China, and a matter to be settled among Chinese alone, Taiwan effectively undercuts any rationale for the international community to come to its aid in a crisis.[2] Since Taiwan's international economic ties are already well developed, the government now reasons that such influence as the island may possess ought to be leveraged for political and security purposes. To the extent that participation in GATT or the Asia-Pacific Economic Cooperation forum (APEC) internationalizes its status in the international arena, even economic IGO participation becomes a key facet of foreign and security policies aimed at leverage and deterrence. Taiwan will likely continue to push for the upgrading of its status in IGOs such as APEC. For while Taiwan's leaders recognize the constraints PRC participation in IGOs places on other members, they nonetheless regard a raised profile as a critical adjunct to the island's broader strategy of deterrence. Indeed, Taiwan's short-term push will probably come in the context of APEC, as the failure to devise a means to invite Lee Teng-hui to Seattle—where Taiwan has friends— much less Jakarta, was badly received across a broad spectrum of local opinion. The UN membership push, though unrealistic, is symbolic of the larger attempt at less ambitious—but, in Taipei's view, achievable—IGO goals.   A higher APEC profile ranks high among these, as does membership in the World Trade Organization (WTO), the successor organization to GATT.

Taipei pursues "flexible" multilateral tactics on two levels. Both are relevant to reunification and status issues:

* *Official Names:* It readily accepts changes of its official name, as well as concurrent seating with Beijing in organizations that already recognize the PRC by *its* official name. A prominent ex-

---

[2]Sutter (1993).

ample was Taiwan's decision to remain in the Asian Development Bank despite the ADB's decision to transfer its "China seat" to Beijing.[3] In 1989, Taiwan sent then-Finance Minister Shirley Kuo to Beijing for the bank's annual meeting, where she stood with fellow delegates for the PRC anthem and for then-President Yang Shangkun's entrance into the meeting hall.

- *Renouncing the Formal China Claim:* Taipei has effectively renounced its claim to sovereignty over China where such claims might stand in the way of the island's entrance into IGOs in its own right. In its GATT application, Taiwan deliberately applied as the "Customs Territory of Taiwan, Penghu, Kinmen, and Matsu," a reference to the territories that Taipei physically controls. This is in part a by-product of peculiarities of the GATT charter, which is geared not to states but rather "governments"—any governments—in a position to raise and lower tariff barriers within the territory they oversee. In this sense, it is surely not in a government's interest to claim responsibility for the tariff behavior of a territory it does not control: no entity wants to be held responsible—and punished—for behavior it can do little to prevent. This goes a long way toward explaining why the Republic of China (ROC) left GATT voluntarily in 1950, even as it retained its United Nations seat and insisted on its China claim in the absolute; it also partly explains why China is willing to allow Taiwan to enter the WTO, albeit subsequent to Beijing's entry.[4]

The flexible IGO strategy, however, especially with respect to name changes, underscores the degree to which Taiwan is now prepared to concede diplomatic form for the substance of a higher international profile. This genuinely concerns Beijing, and rightly so: So flippant a commitment to the ROC claim illustrates how much Taiwan has changed in the past five years. Taipei is increasingly confident that it can assert its identity in the global arena yet keep a cautious eye focused on Beijing. In this sense, the policy of engagement toward the mainland is important: An engaged China, many in Taiwan argue, will likely prove a more accommodating China over the long term. Thus the two prongs of Taipei's foreign policy fall neatly together.

---

[3]Yu (1990).
[4]Ya Qin (1992).

Status and Flexibility in Political Context

Taiwan's flexible policy enjoys virtually universal support on the island. Indeed, the government faces heavy popular pressure to accelerate the pace of this process. In the context of the cross-Strait relationship, however, this pressure is potentially destabilizing. The KMT implicitly offers its version of internationalization as a more realistic alternative to the DPP's push for independence, given the continuing problem of deterring the Chinese threat. Yet public expectations appear so high that the KMT risks the possibility of appearing to Beijing to be little different from the DPP in practice. While the KMT's strategy is no doubt less provocative than the DPP's, it is also risky: China is clearly unhappy with what it views as an attempt by the "Taiwanese" KMT to detach the island from the mainland by a more surreptitious—but no less effective—strategy than the independence-inclined opposition. For this reason, the Chinese have attempted to push the unofficial cross-Strait talks to a higher level by stressing a variety of substantive issues that would anchor Taiwan more closely to the mainland.

Multilateralism and Regional Views

Finally, RAND's interviews elsewhere in Asia revealed that many countries, particularly in Southeast Asia, are prepared to push Beijing, albeit cautiously, for a larger Taiwanese role in regional groupings. And as balancing Taiwan's ambitions with Chinese pressure to exclude it from the global community will no doubt prove difficult, a regional approach to the issue may in fact prove the most workable. RAND's interviews, particularly in Association of Southeast Asian Nations (ASEAN) capitals, indicate an increasing willingness to push for a higher Taiwan profile in economic and commercial regimes, but also a continuing hesitancy with regard to political and security groupings. Underlying these views is a general sense that Taiwan's economic weight and increasing influence, especially as a result of offshore investment trends, may no longer be ignored. If the Taiwanese leverage economic influence for diplomatic gain, such moves may be met warmly in the region provided that Taipei is careful not to push for goals, such as military cooperation or dual recognition, which antagonize Beijing in the extreme. Crosscutting these regional views are a variety of institutional rivalries in various diplomatic and national security establishments. China sections in various foreign ministries, for instance, appear conservative with regard to possible provocations of Beijing. RAND's discussions, however, indicate far greater flexibility in the region on the issue of Taiwan's international role than has hitherto been assumed, and this appears to be a direct result of the influence gained via offshore investment, capital flows, and Taipei's explicit attempt at linkage diplomacy. Broad *regional* consensus has thus emerged that Taiwan's de facto weight in Asia and the Pacific must be recognized; this is balanced, however, by the problem of antagonizing Beijing, which remains constant regionwide, and is exacerbated by outstanding South China Sea disputes.

Conclusion 4

Taiwan is not merely more flexible on issues of status but is increasingly confident in that flexibility. Where Chinese threats once checked independence sentiment, those threats, while palpable, no longer seem so menacing to the island's leadership. Significant foreign exchange reserves (see Figure 3.1), heavy investment in Asian neighbors, the considerable role played by Taiwan capital in many countries, and the benefits in the industrialized world of a democratic image have given Taiwan's leaders a certain confidence in their capacity to cautiously tweak Beijing. While talk of UN membership risks invoking Beijing's wrath, Taiwan's leaders would not speak so brazenly about raising the island's profile if they did not feel confident of their ability to do so. The island's economic power, its leaders reason, gives it a weight that belies its pariah status. Investment and capital flows have therefore become an instrument of Taiwan's diplomacy. The government leverages that power in countries in which Taiwan investment is significant. And Taiwan's key role in the global trading order may "internationalize" its current status: A threat to the "status quo at a minimum," the government reasons, is in some sense a threat to the order of international commerce.

MULTIPLE INTERESTS AND COALITION BUILDING

As three of the above conclusions may potentially prove destabilizing—the emerging consensus in favor of Taiwan's "distinct" identity, "Taiwanization" of the ruling KMT, and increasing confidence in

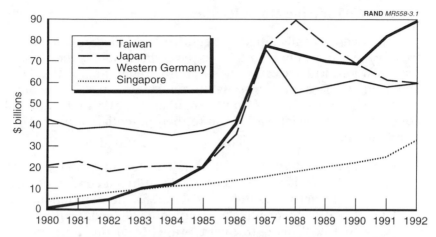

RAND *MR558-3.1*

NOTES: Foreign exchange reserves excluding gold. Figures are end year, except for 1992, which ends in July.
SOURCES: International Monetary Fund (IMF); The Economist Intelligence Unit.
Reprinted by permission from: *The Economist*, October 10, 1992.

Figure 3.1—Foreign Exchange Reserves

Taiwan's ability to leverage wealth and trade for political gain—
Taiwan's increasing diversity, together with the electoral constraints
and incremental nature of the China policy process outlined above,
may in fact come to play a stabilizing role. Though the broad strokes
of a consensus have emerged in Taiwan, the variety of opinion constituencies and—increasingly—policy approaches reinforces the
need to build wide consensus on the island in matters relating to the
status issue and to major shifts in China policy. This is a laborious
process and may check bold, and rash, policy shifts on all sides.
Diversity is manifest within the major parties, among business and
civil groups, and in party-interest group and state-interest group interaction. All of these trends reinforce the need to build policy coalitions and consensus. In the current atmosphere, a major shift in
policy by a narrow party or policy interest may undermine Taiwan's
strengths vis-à-vis the mainland. This trend crosscuts and interacts
with each of the others outlined in this report.

Diversity Within the Major Parties

Directly tied to the dilemma of executive-legislative interaction, as well as the problem of maintaining party discipline, is the issue of party relations with the candidates who run under (nominal) KMT or DPP banners. This cuts across institutional boundaries—as in same-party executive-legislative disputes—and also speaks to the internal coherence of the major parties and to their potential for further factionalization.

- *Party and Candidate:* Institutionally, the candidate-centered campaigns that have emerged in Taiwan breed constituent—as opposed to party-oriented—legislators. The maintenance of legislative discipline in this environment will be difficult for any party that controls both major branches of the government. Taiwan's single-vote, multi-member constituency system rewards any candidate winning the minimum number of required votes in a constituency, and pits candidates of the same party against each other in most electoral districts.[5] This has two consequences for the policy process:

  - Radicals and fringe candidates often run well, and bedrock interest groups can elect many candidates sensitive to their policy concerns provided such sentiment is spread in sufficient minimum numbers across many constituencies, as opposed to being concentrated in a single area.

  - Increasingly, individual candidates are more concerned with guaranteeing that they pass the victory threshold by garnering as many votes as possible than with their party's attempt to spread minimum votes among the maximum number of party candidates in a given district (see Table 3.1). In short, candidate and party objectives often conflict. In multimember constituencies where candidates run against fellow partisans, as well as opposition party candidates, the key to victory for a party apparatus is to spread sufficient numbers of minimum threshold votes among the largest possible number of candidates within a constituency. But Taiwan's nominating system is not rigid, and large numbers of

---

[5]For greater detail, see Nathan (1993).

Table 3.1

Lowest Winning Vote in Territorial Districts, 1992 Legislative Yuan
Elections

District	No. of Seats	No. of Candidates	Total Vote	Lowest Winning Vote	LWV as % of Total Vote
Taipei city N.	9	28	603,766	21,060	3.49
Taipei city S.	9	40	588,930	28,048	4.76
Keelong city	2	5	145,817	37,418	25.66
Yilan county	2	5	207,853	56,005	26.94
Taipei county	16	48	1,390,498	36,845	2.65
Taoyuan county	7	13	628,305	50,279	8.00
Hsinchu county	2	7	185,081	57,231	30.92
Hsinchu city	2	10	136,005	29,810	21.92
Miaoli county	3	10	261,884	56,355	21.52
Taichung county	7	16	616,542	58,501	9.49
Taichung city	4	11	332,624	57,206	17.20
Changhua county	7	16	605,489	59,496	9.83
Nantou county	3	7	243,346	48,253	19.83
Yunlin county	4	8	344,045	49,147	14.29
Chiayi county	3	6	278,353	53,905	19.37
Chiayi city	1	2	116,079	58,145	50.09
Tainan county	5	11	502,215	49,235	9.80
Tainan city	4	13	341,480	50,721	14.85
Kaohsiung county	6	13	534,430	40,252	7.53
Kaohsiung city N.	6	14	350,102	33,027	9.43
Kaohsiung city S.	6	13	306,175	32,456	10.60
Pingtung county	5	11	398,989	48,339	12.12
Taitung county	1	7	67,474	35,657	52.85
Hualien county	2	8	122,928	26,667	21.69
Penghu county	1	3	44,393	20,641	46.50
Lienchiang county	1	2	2,807	1,648	58.71
Chinmen county	1	3	20,531	10,926	53.22

Source: Calculated from *Zili Zaobao* [*Independence Morning News*, Taipei], December 20, 1992, p. 8; *Lianhebao*, December 20, 1992, pp. 3, 9.

Reprinted from *Asian Survey*, Vol. 33, No. 4, April 1993, p. 426.

informally affiliated candidates, who often run well, are on ballots along with official nominees. Many candidates are primarily concerned with their own victories, as opposed to the party's concerns. This undermines a party's ability to spread votes tactically and renders victorious candidates more responsive to the constituents to whom they owe victory than to the party apparatus that now seeks to manage their votes in the legislature.

This has its most significant implications with respect to the China issue: Forging consensus on so contentious an area of public policy requires that parties balance the wide array of sentiment within their ranks: "moderate" and "radical" positions in the DPP, "moderate" and "conservative" ideas in the KMT. And this consensus must be forged among increasingly constituent-oriented legislators.

This jibes neatly with problems of factionalism and consensus-building in the major parties. There exist substantive differences within the KMT on how hard to push Taiwan localism, if at all. In the DPP, party members united by their aversion to KMT rule have managed in the past to hang together in the face of serious internal disputes. But while analysts have often overplayed the DPP's centrifugal tendencies, the party's transition from fringe opposition to potential government may change the stakes internally. The need to think coherently about potential policy alternatives and programs leaves room for substantive, as opposed to personal or political, differences in style to come to the fore. This includes substantive differences over the character of China policy, the means to handle the China interests of DPP constituencies in the business community, and the timing of a formal independence push. Should the DPP take power in Taiwan, certain substantive cleavages are bound to exist and will play out in policy debates. China will no doubt find the prospect of *any* DPP government threatening, but some DPP leaders may prove less inclined than others to challenge Beijing in the short term, and this could have a stabilizing effect on the relationship.

Mainland Investments and Business Influence

The addition of private interests into mainland policy debates complicates political consensus-building efforts. While the Taiwan state's response to the offshore trend in Southeast Asia has been to encourage it, on China investments its policy has largely been reactive. Whatever the parties' political stance toward the mainland, the search for new markets and production cost considerations provide a purely commercial logic to the surge of mainland investments. The state and both major parties thus confront the same two dilemmas with respect to Taiwan's substantial business interests in China:

- To keep industry at home, especially pollution-intensive big industry, requires that the state push legislation with unpopular incentives for firms to retain Taiwan-based production. Pollution and labor concerns must be suppressed, finessed, or coopted. And this must be achieved in a legislative environment that couples lax party discipline with frequent elections, demanding, vocal and increasingly well-organized constituents, and a Byzantine party endorsement system.

- To protect business interests on the mainland requires that both parties be cautious on the status issue. Ironically, it is ethnically Taiwanese enterprise—primarily a core DPP constituency—that drives many of the projects promoting economic integration across the Strait. The DPP, too, worries about economic "dependence" on the mainland; for independence advocates, integration with the Chinese economy can act only as a check on future moves in that direction. Both parties thus confront the same dilemma: how not to alienate old constituencies in the powerful business community while at the same time keeping an eye focused on Taiwan's security needs. This dilemma cuts across ethnic cleavages. For Taiwan's mainlanders, investment couples a potential integratory check on independence sentiment with a variety of complex security issues. For ethnic Taiwanese, it matches lucrative commercial opportunities with the problem of economic dependence and long-range checks on the potential to move toward de jure independence. Both major parties, and both major ethnicities, must come to terms with similar dilemmas.

Conclusion 5

Taiwan has become a more complex place than it was under the civil war generation. This has profound implications for the way in which China policy filters through the domestic debate. Where one interest—the KMT's—once defined the issue, and two interests—the KMT's and the DPP's—eventually supplanted the old approach, multiple interests on the island now have distinct and often conflicting stakes in Taiwan's mainland policy. Internal divisions in the

KMT over the status issue muddy the party's policy: Which KMT determines the prevailing line? Bolder as well as "go slow" politicians similarly muddy the DPP's position: All DPP supporters back independence, but at what pace? Not all DPP politicians are so willing to openly test the credibility of Beijing's threat. Moreover, Taiwan's powerful business community is divided between the many firms that now have mainland investments to protect, and others whose production remains on the island and who must compete with mainland, and mainland-relocated Taiwanese, firms. Many of Taiwan's mainland competitors are situated in precisely those industries that have benefited from Taiwan investment.[6] Taiwan's China policy will not merely be constrained by electoralism and public opinion but will thus increasingly be shaped by coalition building. One coalition might bring flexible KMT and more moderate DPP leaders together. Another might pit mainland-invested business with the KMT against those in the DPP who advocate a more provocative approach. A third could bring protection-oriented business into alignment with independence advocates in the DPP. Finally, the emergence in the past year of a third political party—the New Party—dominated by second-generation mainlander defectors from the KMT complicates the electoral math and may further muddy the process of coalition building.

---

[6]See Yen (1991).

Chapter Four

ECONOMIC TRENDS: TRADE DEPENDENCE, OFFSHORE INVESTMENT, AND INDUSTRIAL RESTRUCTURING

A number of trends aggregate into one broad conclusion.

Trade Dependence, Offshore Expansion, and Industrial Restructuring: The combination of trade dependence, accelerating offshore investment, and the slow pace of restructuring the domestic economy to a more capital-intensive focus militate in favor of an emphasis on continued stability and non-conflict in the Strait and in Taiwan's trade relationships. Unless the island is prepared to jettison its focus on the very issues most crucial to its long-term economic well-being, the need not to provoke a conflict will combine with the constraints associated with deterrence to militate in favor of non-conflict.

TRADE DEPENDENCE, OFFSHORE EXPANSION, AND INDUSTRIAL RESTRUCTURING

The Common Solution to a Two-Faced Dilemma

While *patterns* of trade are beginning to shift as Taiwan increases the intra-regional share of its exports, the island continues to rely on export trade as a primary source of economic growth. For this reason, its loss of comparative advantage in low-wage labor may prove disastrous absent significant industrial restructuring, for it is ballooning wage rates, together with other constraints, that have driven Taiwan business offshore in search of raw materials, new markets, and a lower-cost production process. In fact, this confronts the interest groups associated with two dilemmas—dependence on China, and the loss of competitiveness to lower wage rivals—with what amounts to the same problem: how to restructure the Taiwan economy away from a labor-intensive to a capital- and technology-intensive basis. For though much of the offshore movement has been to Southeast Asia, China has become a key recipient of Taiwan investment, and this inevitably has political ramifications. To those who worry about economic "dependence" and its political consequences, the strongest possible check on such trends is the restructuring of Taiwan's economy toward a capital-intensive, technology-driven base that compensates for the loss of low-wage, labor-intensive industry to the mainland. Given labor and cost considerations, meanwhile, such restructuring provides a solution to the specifically economic problems associated with slipping comparative advantage, business flight, the acceleration of the offshore trend, and the imperatives of long-range economic competitiveness. Checking China and sustaining economic growth thus crucially depend upon elements of the same process: Taiwan's capacity to make the transition to a new place in the region's division of labor.

Offshore Investment and Mainland Interests

Though initial cross-Strait contact was grounded in the variety of domestic pressures in Taiwan—KMT and army veterans' desire to visit relatives, etc.—the commercial underpinnings of "mainland fever" are in fact grounded in the structural dilemmas described in the last paragraph. In the face of wage push demands, as well as social pressures such as those from a nascent environmental movement, Taiwan's labor- and pollution-intensive industry, particularly export-oriented light industry, has been effectively outcompeted by rivals in Thailand, Indonesia, China, and elsewhere: production sites with lower land and labor costs, comparatively lax environmental standards, and an array of investment incentives and tax breaks. Taiwan lost some portion of this comparative advantage in part because domestic reforms at home led to the emergence of autonomous interests outside the formal corporatist structure of state controls, particularly in the area of labor organization. The link between offshore production and exports in such areas as machines, equipment, and industrial materials, however, provides a purely

economic rationale.[1]   Taken together, Taiwan's light industry—
footwear, toys, garments, etc.—had already begun to move offshore
to Southeast Asia by the time the state's more liberal mainland policies took effect: Taiwan firms have risked more than US$15 billion in
Southeast Asian investments and are the largest single source of investment in Vietnam (see Figure 4.1).[2]

But China has had particular allure for two reasons: a common
language and culture, coupled with special incentives for "Taiwan

RAND *MR558-4.1*

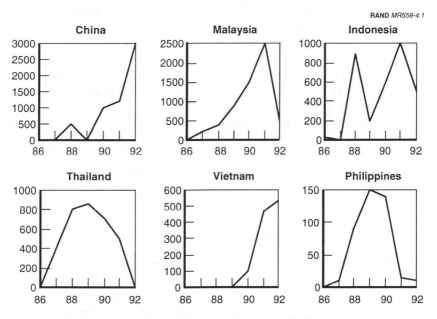

NOTES: Figures illustrate direct investment in US$millions. Indonesian
figures for 1992 reflect January–September. Philippines figures for 1992 reflect
January–October.
   SOURCES: Ministry of Economic Affairs and Chung-hua Institution for
Economic Research, Taipei.
   Reprinted by permission from: *Far Eastern Economic Review*, March 18,
1993, p. 45.

Figure 4.1—Taiwan's Approved Direct Investment in Various Countries

---

[1]Schive (1992), p. 117.

[2]*FEER,* March 18, 1993, pp. 44–50.

compatriots," make negotiations and management easier than in many countries; also, the lure of China's huge domestic market provides a powerful incentive for Taiwan firms to seek a toehold. More importantly, "wages in countries such as Thailand and Malaysia, [once] one-tenth of those in Taiwan [are] now only one-fifth to one-third cheaper, while China offers differentials close to what was available in Southeast Asia" in 1988.[3] The trend has thus been for Taiwan light industry to move production facilities to the "cheap labor, lax environmental standards" environment offered by the Chinese. Where *raw materials* and cost considerations provided incentive for moves to Southeast Asia in the 1980s, the search for *new markets* and cost considerations impels business to look to China in the 1990s. With the exception of Vietnam—where the reform experiment and the foreign trade infrastructure are less developed than in China—mainland investments provide a number of cushions and benefits that Southeast Asian investments do not. And the primary brakes on China investment—political risk, potential fallout from deteriorating U.S.-China relations (Most-Favored Nation (MFN)-type sanctions would badly hurt Taiwan exports originating in mainland factories), and government reluctance in Taiwan—have less to do with cost considerations than with tectonic political and diplomatic shifts.

While the Taiwan state's response to the offshore trend in Southeast Asia has been to encourage it, on China investments its policy has largely been reactive. Whatever the KMT's political stance toward the mainland, there is a purely commercial logic that impels Taiwan business to look to China as an offshore production site and poten-tial market. But to a state, much less the opposition DPP, that wor-ries about long-range economic dependence and Chinese leverage over Taiwan business, investments in the PRC mix political and security risks with the lucrative commercial opportunities they offer. Investment and trade bans have thus been peeled away by an almost grudging state largely in ex post recognition of the fait accompli of trade via third parties or in prohibited products. The state's inability to stem the tide is reflected in the fact that exports to China, which the state had sought to limit to a threshold of 10 percent, are now estimated to range between 13 percent and 18 percent of Taiwan's

---

[3]*FEER*, March 18, 1993, p. 45.

gross exports.[4] Over the first eleven months of 1993, indirect trade through Hong Kong was up 19.1 percent to US$7.91 billion. And with direct trade factored into this equation, total two-way trade over the same period amounted to some US$13.85 billion, estimated to rise to nearly US$14 billion when December figures are factored in; by any standard, this represents an enormous increase over the US$7.41 billion two-way trade total for 1992 (see Figures 4.2–4.4).

The extraordinary scale and ever-increasing pace of this integration inevitably make a political problem out of investment matters. As noted above, interests around this issue are complex and cut across political and ethnic cleavages. For Taiwan's mainlanders, investment couples integratory checks on independence with the complex security issues associated with economic dependence; for ethnic Taiwanese, it matches lucrative commercial opportunities in a setting of slipping competitiveness with the problems economic dependence will raise for the potential to move toward de jure political independence. Given that most offshore investment capital

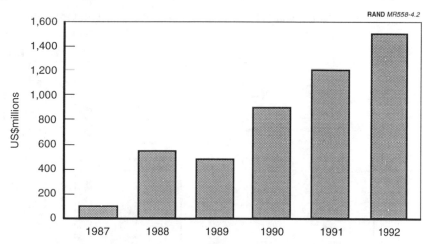

SOURCE: Chung-hua Institution for Economic Research.
Reprinted by permission from: *Far Eastern Economic Review*, September 17, 1992, p. 23.

Figure 4.2—Taiwan Investment in China

---

[4] *FEER*, May 20, 1993, p. 66.

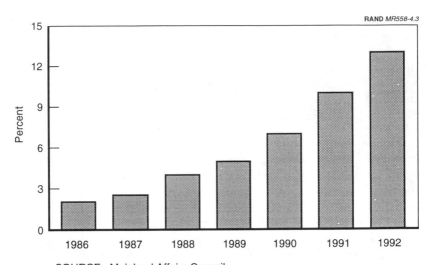

SOURCE: Mainland Affairs Council.
Reprinted by permission from: *Far Eastern Economic Review*, May 20, 1993, p. 66.

Figure 4.3—Taiwan's Exports to China as Share of Total Exports

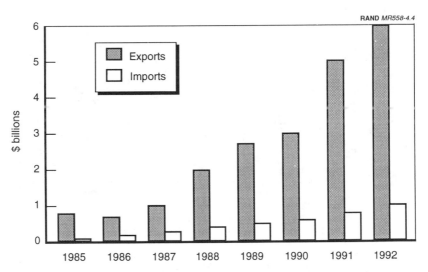

SOURCE: National Statistics (1992 figures are forecast estimates).
Reprinted by permission from: *The Economist*, October 10, 1992.

Figure 4.4—Taiwan's Trade with China

originates from ethnically Taiwanese sources, the DPP's position is particularly precarious; this raises interesting issues of intra-Taiwanese elite dynamics and cuts directly across debates surrounding local ethnicity. Moreover, surveys by Taiwan economists show that light industry moves to the mainland frequently serve to drive from business that portion of light industry that remains in Taiwan.

As the Taiwan economist Yen Tzung-ta points out: "Taiwan products are facing severe competition from those made in China. And what's more, the products chiefly involved in the competition are precisely those which Taiwan-funded companies in mainland China are producing—toys, footwear, textiles, garments, hardware, and aquatic products, etc." Thus, argues Yen, as the number of Taiwan-funded companies on the mainland increases, this trend's impact on what remains of Taiwan's light industrial base is likely to grow worse.[5] That raises the prospect, proposed by some in Taiwan, of state assistance to local enterprise challenged by Taiwan-invested or Taiwan-owned offshore competitors. As noted above, such assistance might pit business interest against business interest and leave the Taiwan state—embedded in a system in which money politics, and hence business influence, is significant—caught uncomfortably in between.

All of these economic strands undoubtedly render local industrial restructuring more imperative and reinforce the need to create conditions conducive to that process: long-term stability, secure trade and capital flows, and participation in the accelerating process of regional economic and commercial integration.

State-Led Restructuring

Interestingly, Taiwan already has separate China policies for labor-intensive and capital-intensive industry. These are intended to keep the latter on the island while recognizing absolute limitations on the state's capacity to retain local light industrial plant. Continued emphasis on the capital side, with gradual movement into high technology areas may provide the state some leverage against China-invested light industrial interests over the long haul and strengthen

---

[5]Yen (1991), p. 41.

its position in the coalition process described above. Should ever-larger proportions of the workforce and capital move into high technology sectors, the cost to the state of offending China-invested light or even old heavy industrial interests may be reduced. The creation of science and technology parks, together with the government's high technology development emphasis, must therefore be read as attempts to alter the current pattern of crosscutting economic interests and policy dynamics. To the state, industrial policy is the logical corollary to strategic and foreign policies aimed at deterrence of the Chinese and the internationalization of Taiwan's status.

Yet as one recent commentator points out, while extant technological assets and a base for strategic alliances place Taiwan in an advantageous position, the "forces of technological protectionism"—questions about the "viability of alliance building," and the issues of "trust, cross-cultural understanding, and politics" associated with strategic partnering—confront the island's development planners with real problems. Further, "there are major information and skills barriers confronting Taiwan in terms of the adoption of new technologies such as informatics. Even in the industrialized West, where computers have become extremely popular, the fact remains that utilization rates are extremely low. This suggests that without an enhanced infrastructure or adequate training programs, Taiwan is likely to have similar if not worse problems with assimilating many of the newer technologies. It is one thing for Taiwan to desire to get beyond Original Equipment Manufacturer (OEM) status and enter into both product and process design on a regular basis; it is another thing to succeed at doing them well. While there clearly is a strong foundation on Taiwan that suggests a high potential for success, the reality is that the dynamics of global competition call for a type of technological responsiveness and flexibility that may or may not be present in view of the existing industrial structure. On the whole, Taiwan's firms may be too small to provide the constant stream of investment needed to keep pace with global technological changes."[6] For these reasons, industrial restructuring demands a long-range commitment to overall stability. And the centrality of technology-based restructuring to Taiwan's economic future is blind to political partisanship.

----

[6]Simon (1992), p. 144.

Moreover, the Taiwan government has coupled industrial restructuring with a broader effort to diversify the island's economic base. To control for the possibility of "overdependence" on China, the government hopes to convert the island into a regional base of operations for transnational corporations. This involves a significant attempt to upgrade Taiwan's commercial and communications infrastructure, including facilities and ports supporting air and sea links, financial and telecommunications services and "facilities for manufacturing high-value products." Yet, as Ralph Clough points out, "this program also presents a dilemma, for it cannot be successful unless Taiwan opens direct air and sea transportation to mainland China. Thus in order to increase the stake of foreign corporations in Taiwan, improving its survivability in the face of PRC pressures, it must tie itself more closely by air and sea to the PRC, increasing the channels by which PRC pressure could be exerted."[7]

Conclusion 6

The combination of trade dependence, accelerating offshore investment, and the slow pace of restructuring the domestic economy to a more capital-intensive focus militate in favor of an emphasis on continued stability and non-conflict in the Strait and in Taiwan's trade relationships. Any conflict between Taiwan and China would automatically involve the region as a whole: The disruption of regional stability would severely affect the commercial ties of both protagonists—but particularly Taiwan, given its very high level of trade dependence—interrupt regionwide capital flows, and disrupt the general trend toward regional commercial integration. Moreover, as inter-Asian trade bulks increasingly large in the region's total commercial picture and as Taiwan, no less than China, is a major actor in this drama, any Strait dispute would severely skew the distribution of resources, and the policy focus, away from critical economic issues. Both Taiwan and China would be forced to grant priority access to resources to the military. In Taiwan's case, however, the skew would be virtually total: Transport infrastructure would no doubt be commandeered for military use, the security of

---

[7]Personal communication, October 26, 1994. For elaboration, see *Free China Journal*, May 27, 1994, p. 7.

Taiwan's shipping would be placed in doubt, and commercial, trade and crucial restructuring issues would automatically be relegated to backburner status. Taiwan investments in China would be placed under threat: Chinese firms that benefit from Taiwan capital, technology, and skill would lose continued access, while Taiwan assets might well be lost. Finally, the party that initiated outright conflict and is perceived internationally as the provocateur might face a variety of sanctions designed to punish, and potentially reverse, its behavior. In this context, stability is important to both protagonists from a purely economic standpoint but is especially important to Taiwan. The island's continuing trade dependence and the slow pace of industrial restructuring demand stability over a relatively long period. Unless Taiwan is prepared to jettison its focus on the very issues most crucial to its long-term economic well-being, the need not to provoke a conflict will combine with the constraints associated with deterrence to militate in favor of non-conflict.

Chapter Five

IMPLICATIONS AND POSSIBLE SCENARIOS

Collectively, these trends make clear that Taiwan and the Taiwan-China relationship are in some sense moving targets. The island walks a fine line between guaranteeing and enhancing its position on one hand, and deterring Beijing on the other. That dilemma must undoubtedly be faced down by whichever party or coalition of interests attains power. Indeed, because Beijing's policy is the wild card in this dispute, the credibility of the Chinese threat is a dilemma that any Taiwan government, whether KMT or DPP, will have to face down. For now, the need to walk that line is the most basic hazard of incumbency: The KMT must do so, while the DPP snipes from opposition. But the Chinese threat would be even more palpable should a DPP government eventually attain power, and given the need to deter the Chinese, an actual DPP government might well choose to accommodate long-term ambitions to the imperatives of effective deterrence, at least in the short-term.

Three potential scenarios capture this tension between action and deterrence. Since the Taiwan-China relationship will either continue to steadily evolve or receive a sudden jolt, the three scenarios address each possibility in light of the report's six summary conclusions:

1. The apparent emergence of broad consensus in favor of Taiwan's de facto, though not necessarily de jure, independence.

2. The ruling KMT's effort to accommodate itself to the local constraints associated with this consensus.

3. The institutional and electoral checks that prevent any party from upsetting this status quo without first forging broad-based islandwide support for change.

4. Increasing confidence in Taiwan of the island's ability to leverage wealth, investment, and trade for international political gain.

5. The pluralization of Taiwan society into interests that share that confidence, but that hold divergent views as to how this might best be accomplished.

6. The ongoing attempt to restructure Taiwan's economy in the direction of capital- and technology-intensive, as opposed to labor-intensive, industry such that the island's dependence on offshore production—and especially on mainland investment—need not be coupled with vulnerability to the whims of offshore partners.

A forthcoming RAND report focusing on Chinese security policy addresses the potential for an unprecipitated PRC move against Taiwan. As this report is primarily concerned with Taiwan's foreign and security behavior, the scenarios below suggest circumstances under which Taiwan could initiate a sudden change in the relationship; the result of any such decision would almost certainly be conflictual. Alternatively, steady, but incremental, movement in the relationship could produce either conflict or continued non-conflictual evolution.

SCENARIO 1: SUDDEN CHANGE, INITIATED BY TAIWAN

The most likely Taiwan-initiated jolt to the relationship would be an outright declaration of de jure independence. But given the current approach to this issue of both the KMT and the New Party, in the short term only a single party DPP government could possibly precipitate this. Moreover, since the DPP has made independence an explicit plank of its platform, China will undoubtedly regard any DPP victory as genuine cause for alarm and increase the tone of its threats, and the substance of potential pressure, as soon as a DPP electoral victory is assured. In this context, four factors militate against the possibility of an independence declaration:

- The Chinese threat to resort to force in the event of an independence declaration is clear, explicit, and is continually restated in the press and by Chinese political and military figures. Since a DPP government, as opposed to mere opposition, would be charged with deterring threats to the island's security, an out-right independence declaration might well be deemed too provocative in the short term.

- Given the Chinese threat, DPP politicians are themselves split on the precise timing and nature of a move toward formal independence. Not all DPP politicians doubt the credibility of the Chinese threat or place faith in the possibility of outside—especially U.S.—assistance in the event of conflict. Indeed one prominent DPP politician told RAND that a DPP electoral victory would itself be regarded by some in the party as tantamount to a declaration of the island's independence. By this logic, no formal declaration would be required; but it need not be pointed out that this rendering leaves room for future compromise, as well as a subsequent DPP defeat and renewed KMT rule.

- While public opinion in Taiwan surely does not favor reunification on Beijing's terms, if at all, a declaration that provoked Beijing to action might well be viewed by the Taiwan populace as irresponsible. At this time, few Taiwanese appear prepared to risk the substance of de facto independence for the legal guarantees of de jure independence by testing Beijing's will to make good its threat (see Table 5.1).

- Given KMT and New Party opposition, the DPP would almost certainly have to fully control both the executive and legislative branches of government to make a declaration substantively effective and politically compelling. Since it is yet unclear precisely what leverage will be available to the opposition in the evolving legislative process, the emergence of genuine levers for the expression of opposition sentiment might allow the KMT and the New Party to resist or block DPP initiatives.

SCENARIO 2: STEADY EVOLUTION, A CONFLICTUAL OUTCOME

As noted in the section on pluralization in Chapter Three, the emerging diversity of interests in Taiwan's China policy process may require that policymakers increasingly rely on coalition building with respect to mainland policy. This constraint, together with the probable need to forge wide popular consensus on any initiative that

Table 5.1

Public Opinion on Taiwan Independence Movement

Date	Survey Conductor	Approve/ Disapprove (%)
November 1988	PORF[a]	2/—
August 1989	PORF	16/—
December 1989	PORF	8.2/—
June 1990	PORF	12.5/67.0
October 1990	*Lianhebao*	21/57
December 1990	PORF	12.0/61.7
June 1991	PORF	12.7/65.3
September 1991	*Lianhebao*	18/54
October 1991	*Lianhebao*	14/58
October 1992	PORF	15.1/63.3
October 1992	*Lianhebao*	16/51
March 1993	*Lianhebao*	17/49
May 1993	PORF	23.7/55.3

[a]PORF: Public Opinion Research Foundation.

Sources: *Mainland Policy: Selected Opinion Polls Conducted in Taiwan 1988–92*, Mainland Affairs Council, The Executive Yuan, Taipei, Republic of China, August 1992, p. 6; *Zhongyang ribao* [*Central Daily News*, Taipei], 1 November 1992, p. 1; 11 May 1993, p. 1, data provided by the Public Opinion Poll Centre of the *Lianhebao*.

Reprinted from *China Quarterly*, No. 136, December 1993, p. 829.

would significantly alter the status quo, means that Taiwan will almost certainly attempt to strengthen its distinct profile in a manner that avoids antagonizing Beijing. This will especially be the case in the absence of outright DPP control of both the executive and legislative branches of government. It may not, however, prove acceptable to Beijing over the long term. None among the current political trends in Taiwan is likely to be viewed on the mainland as reassuring. The DPP has gained strength since 1986 and, despite recent setbacks at the local level, has emerged as a genuine contender for power and a potential majority party. The KMT is no longer unified behind, or explicitly committed to, the "One China" approach. Finally, the predominantly second generation mainlander New Party, though publicly committed to reunification, derives support primarily on the basis of populist issues such as corruption and the power of money to influence the political process. Because this element of local populism belies the New Party's stand on reunification issues, though many mainlanders may eventually support it and drift away from the Taiwanese-led KMT, given Taiwan's ethnic breakdown the party will have to draw support from among ethnic Taiwanese to increase its influence in the years ahead. None of these trends is likely to be viewed positively in Beijing. Even KMT victories will be regarded with a jaundiced eye. With "One China" advocates increasingly marginalized in Taiwan's political process, Beijing may feel compelled to arrest what it views as the possible institutionalization of the division the longer it persists. Since so few among local political trends in Taiwan are encouraging from Beijing's vantage point, impatience with the pace of strictly political, as opposed to commercial, integration and change may prod China's leaders to decisive action.

SCENARIO 3: STEADY EVOLUTION, POSSIBLE NON-CONFLICTUAL OUTCOMES

Parallel to these political trends is the fact of increasing economic integration and interdependence across the Strait. Investment and interdependence may in fact serve to stabilize the relationship. Since trade and investment are, in the main, mutually beneficial, and since China remains preoccupied with issues of modernization and succession, continued evolution of the economic and exchange relationship may forestall any short- to medium-term conflict. Over the longer term, a generally stable evolution of the relationship might produce one of three possible outcomes.

- Given Taiwan's size and trade dependence, as well as China's extraordinary potential for continued growth, interdependence could increasingly tie Taiwan to its mainland investments. By this logic, interdependence and complementarity between the two economies will evolve into Taiwan's dependence as China's continued growth levels the playing field and gives China a variety of alternative, including domestic, sources of development capital, investment, and technology. In this scenario, China's relative weight, and the scope of Taiwan's dependence, would allow the Chinese to dictate terms.

- Alternatively, increasing economic integration may render the reunification issue moot and make reunification a "natural" outcome of the process of interdependence and mutual benefit:

Genuine interdependence might open a window for political re-unification to occur of its own accord. Both the KMT and DPP leaderships worry about precisely this eventuality. For this reason, the government has attempted to promote Southeast Asian investments as an alternative to opportunities in China, and to check the possibility of long-range economic dependence.

- Long-term integration, interdependence, and stability might build mutual trust, pacify China's leadership, or dampen popular enthusiasm on the mainland for an "absolutist" position on the Taiwan question. In this scenario, long-term stability and continuing evolution of the relationship need not lead to "natural" reunification. Rather, they would allow Taiwan to declare independence on the basis of a history of mutual trust, and in a manner that would control for the harsh reaction likely in response to some form of Scenario 1.

A final possibility, which raises entirely separate issues for U.S. policy, is that in the event of domestic strife in China, Taiwan's leaders might seize the opportunity to declare independence. This reckoning, however, crosscuts issues and constraints raised in the companion RAND report on Chinese foreign and security policy.

Given the underlying themes of this report's six summary conclusions, a degree of stability seems likely in the short to medium term. For in the main, the trends that underlie these conclusions suggest that a broad-based consensus, and wide coalitions, will need to be built to effect politically compelling, and substantively enduring, change in the most contentious arenas of Taiwan's public policy process. Nowhere is this more likely than with respect to mainland policy and the local debate over Taiwan's status. Rhetoric, policy, and politics will continuously interact.

Three conclusions thus reflect trends that are potentially destabilizing and appear to be pulling Taiwan away from any substantive commitment to reunification: the political and social changes associated with emerging consensus in favor of a "distinct" Taiwan identity; "Taiwanization" of the ruling KMT; and increasing confidence in Taiwan's ability to leverage wealth, investment, and trade for ambitious foreign policy goals. Three additional conclusions reflect stabilizing trends: constraints on bold policy shifts imposed by

Taiwan's electoral system; the emergence of plural, and potentially conflicting, local interests; and continuing economic integration with the mainland. Coupled with security and deterrence issues, these stabilizing trends suggest four key constraints on Taiwan's foreign and security policy process:

- The Chinese threat and the imperatives of effective deterrence

- The need to forge wide consensus to effect a major shift in China policy

- The diversity of interests complicating the coalition and consensus-building process

- Taiwan's continuing trade dependence and the rapid expansion of offshore investment.

Taken together, these constraints exert powerful pressure on *all* parties in Taiwan not to upset the delicate balance in the cross-Strait relationship. But as noted above, China's own policy toward Taiwan remains something of a wild card. Furthermore, local worries about long-range economic dependence and more complete economic integration may intertwine with such destabilizing trends as the emerging consensus in favor of a distinct Taiwan identity. This could push independence advocates to view their window of opportunity as closing so long as the present integratory trends persist. In the short to medium term, these four constraints will likely preclude rash moves by the Taiwan side, but if Taiwan does unilaterally jolt the relationship, all bets on China's response are off. Fear and distrust of Chinese motives is palpable in Taiwan. Even in an atmosphere of increasing pride and confidence, many Taiwanese are deeply cynical about the island's longer-term prospects and suggest that Taiwan will be unable to retain even a modicum of independence over the long term given the accelerating pace of economic integration. Though this cynicism depresses Taiwan's friends, it may nonetheless reflect a view that provocation is no way to guarantee Taiwan's distinct identity in light of China's probable response. Yet it also means that the stakes for independence diehards will continue to rise as this long-term process of economic and social integration with the mainland continues apace. And the boldest among these may perceive a need to ratchet up the pressure before it is "too late" to do so. Such a development would have a severe impact on the cross-Strait relationship, and the Chinese response to more intense local discussion of these issues will likely prove harsh. Without a doubt, the intensity of that discussion will in fact increase; but reconciling public discourse in a democracy with the security threats that are the by-product of that discussion will be Taiwan's primary challenge in the period immediately ahead.

Chapter Six

TRENDS TO WATCH: CHANGE AND THE THREE SCENARIOS

SCENARIO 1: SUDDEN CHANGE, INITIATED BY TAIWAN

Since a DPP majority government appears prerequisite to this scenario at the present time, the party's future electoral fortunes will be important to watch, especially in the run-up to direct presidential elections in 1996, the first opportunity the DPP will have to field a candidate for Taiwan's highest office. Moreover, with elements of the KMT increasingly flexible on the status issue, some type of KMT-DPP convergence might be feasible in the event of a decisive shift in public opinion toward independence sentiment, and given the continuing process of leadership transition in the KMT; this is especially the case in light of the potential for factional rivalry in the two major parties.

Events in China could also play a role in precipitating this scenario. Should China descend into chaos in the post-Deng transition period, a number of pro-independence groups in Taiwan might view the mainland's woes as Taiwan's opportunity. Additionally, the development of links between Taiwan and mainland coastal provinces, particularly Fujian, may create a constituency sympathetic to Taiwan's concerns and give the island breathing space in the event that internal Chinese debates over the Taiwan issue turn confrontational.

On the diplomatic front, Taiwan's leaders will undoubtedly press the international community for greater recognition of Taiwan's "distinct" status. The DPP approves of this process for reasons of its own, and as the process accelerates—should Taiwan be successful in its continuing quest for a raised profile—certain groups in Taiwan may come to believe that the island's distinct status has become sufficiently institutionalized in the global community to provide a basis for, and a constituency in support of, a formal move toward de jure independence.

Of course, this trend will always be checked by the imperatives of deterrence: constraints outlined in the companion report on China militate against *unprovoked* Chinese action, but *provoked* action is another matter entirely in light of the degree to which the Chinese threat of force is continually, and explicitly, restated. Should Taiwan declare independence, the possibility that China would make good its threat seems high given the importance of the Taiwan question domestically and the loss of face that would be associated with a failure to respond to a unilateral declaration.

SCENARIO 2: STEADY EVOLUTION, A CONFLICTUAL OUTCOME

Continuing "progress" in the unofficial cross-Strait talks is important to the Chinese leadership, which has expressed displeasure at what it views as the slow pace, and lack of concrete "results," of the dialogue. At one level, this is a function of divergent attitudes about the process. To the Chinese, who refuse to accept a dialogue that places Taiwan on an equal footing with the PRC, these talks are viewed as the first step along the road to eventual reunification. But given the CCP's recent acceptance of the "Taiwan authorities," rather than the KMT per se, as its interlocutor on the island, China's leaders no longer appear to rely on the notion of a third CCP-KMT united front as the basis for future discussions but accept that "both sides can discuss any subject, including the modality of negotiations, the question of what parties, groups and personalities may participate as well as any other matters of concern to the Taiwan side" in their "contacts and negotiations."[1] Taiwan prefers to regard the talks as a dialogue between equals, an implicit bow to its argument for a dis-

---

[1] PRC White Paper on Taiwan. This important policy document has been translated into English in FBIS, China, September 1, 1993, p. 48.

tinct local identity, and a rhetorical, as well as practical, stumbling-block to future compromise and discussion.

Given these divergent views—in some sense, a divergent approach to the very idea, purpose, and utility of a dialogue—as well as Beijing's displeasure at virtually all of the political trends in Taiwan, the Chinese reaction to each round of talks must be closely monitored. To a mainland leadership that sees so many dangers in Taiwan's drift toward localism and rule by younger, ethnically Taiwanese leaders, the pace of progress in the Strait dialogue, as well as of economic integration, is fundamentally important: the longer the separation continues, many on the mainland reason, the more likely that it will become institutionalized and therefore permanent. Dissatisfaction with the pace of integration and dialogue might precipitate some type of Chinese policy shift.

SCENARIO 3: STEADY EVOLUTION, POSSIBLE NON-CONFLICTUAL OUTCOMES

Finally, given the high price of conflict for both protagonists, as well as the constraints outlined above, this scenario appears most likely in the short to medium term.

But integration is fraught with dangers for Taiwan. Leaders of both major parties worry that unless the island can shift its economic focus to emphasize indigenous high technology enterprise, the offshore trend may evolve into a dependent relationship as China's continuing growth levels the economic and commercial playing field. In this context, any attempt by the Chinese to link cross-Strait economic issues to shifts in the two sides' political relationship should be closely monitored. Given Taiwan's size and trade dependence, such linkage could presage an attempt by Beijing to manipulate the island's weaknesses for political gain. Linkage might provide a means to ratchet up the level of Chinese pressure.

BIBLIOGRAPHY

Bosco, Joseph, "Taiwan Factions: Guanxi, Patronage and the State in Local Politics," in Murray Rubenstein, ed., *The Other Taiwan: 1945 to the Present.* Armonk, NY: ME Sharpe, 1994.

Cheng Hsiao-shih, *Party-Military Relations in the PRC and Taiwan: Paradoxes of Control.* Boulder, CO: Westview Press, 1990.

Cheng Tun-jen and Stephan Haggard, eds., *Political Change in Taiwan.* Boulder, CO: Lynne Rienner Publishers, 1992.

Clough, Ralph N., *Reaching Across the Taiwan Strait: People-to-People Diplomacy.* Boulder, CO: Westview Press, 1993.

Copper, John, *Taiwan's 1991 and 1992 Non-Supplemental Elections: Reaching a Higher Stage of Democracy.* Lanham, MD: University Press of America, 1994.

Fic, Victor, "Taiwan's Air Force: Redefining ROCAF and National Defense," *Asian Defense Journal,* August 1993.

Godwin, Paul H. B., "The Use of Military Force Against Taiwan: Potential PRC Scenarios," in Parris H. Chang and Martin Lasater, eds., *If China Crosses the Taiwan Strait: The International Response.* Lanham, MD: University Press of America, 1993, pp. 15–33.

"Guomindang gexin: mei xinxin, Minjindang zhizheng: bu fangxin; liangdang jingzheng: minyi diaocha" [No confidence in KMT innovation, unease about the DPP in power; the two-party competition: a survey of popular views], *Tianxia* [*Commonwealth*, Taipei], July 1, 1993, pp. 136–143.

"Haixia liang'an de junhuo maimai: zhuanti" [The weapons trade on the two sides of the Strait: a special report], *Jiushi niandai* [*The Nineties*, Hong Kong], May 1991, pp. 51–63.

Hickey, Denis van-Vranken, *US-Taiwan Security Ties: From Cold War to Beyond Containment.* Westport, CT: Praeger, 1994.

Nathan, Andrew J., "The Legislative Yuan Elections in Taiwan: Consequences of the Electoral System," *Asian Survey.* Vol. 37, No. 4, April 1993, pp. 424–438.

Qin Ya, "GATT Membership for Taiwan: An Analysis in International Law," *International Law and Politics,* Vol. 24, 1992, pp. 1059–1105.

Rubenstein, Murray, *The Other Taiwan: 1945 to the Present.* Armonk, NY: ME Sharpe, 1994.

Schive, Chi, "Taiwan's Emerging Position in the International Division of Labor," in Denis Fred Simon and Michael Y. M. Kau, eds., *Taiwan: Beyond the Economic Miracle.* Armonk, NY: ME Sharpe, 1992, pp. 101–122.

Simon, Denis Fred, "Taiwan's Emerging Technological Trajectory: Creating New Forms of Comparative Advantage," in Denis Fred Simon and Michael Y. M. Kau, eds., *Taiwan: Beyond the Economic Miracle.* Armonk, NY: ME Sharpe, 1992, pp. 123–150.

Sutter, Robert G., "The United States and the Changing East Asian Order: Implications for Taiwan's Ability to Deter Possible Threats from the Mainland," in Parris H. Chang and Martin Lasater, eds., *If China Crosses the Taiwan Strait: The International Response.* Lanham, MD: University Press of America, 1993, pp. 99–119.

"Taiwan junhuo cong nali lai?" [Where Does Taiwan's Weaponry Come From?], *Jiushi niandai* [*The Nineties*, Hong Kong], December 1990, pp. 52–67.

Tien Hung-mao, "Transformation of an Authoritarian Party-State: Taiwan's Development Experience," in Tun-jen Cheng and

Stephan Haggard, eds., *Political Change in Taiwan.* Boulder, CO: Lynne Rienner Publishers, 1992, pp. 33–55.

Ts'ai Ling and Ramon H. Myers, "Surviving the Rough and Tumble of Presidential Politics in an Emerging Democracy: The 1990 Elections in the Republic of China on Taiwan," *China Quarterly,* No. 129, March 1992, pp. 123–148.

Yen Tzung-ta, "Taiwan Investment in Mainland China and Its Impact on Taiwan's Industries," *Issues and Studies,* May 1991, pp. 10–42.

Yu, Peter Kien-hong, "On Taipei's Rejoining the Asian Development Bank (ADB) Subsequent to Beijing's Entry: One Country, Two Seats?" *Asian Affairs,* Vol. 17, No. 1, Spring 1990, pp. 3–13.